3rd International Workshop for Computational Linguistics of Uralic Languages (IWCLUL 2017)

St. Petersburg, Russia
23 – 24 January 2017

ISBN: 978-1-5108-3665-5

Introduction

Uralic is an interesting group of languages from the computational-linguistic perspective. The Uralic languages share large parts of morphological and morphophonological complexity that is not present in the Indo-European language family, which has traditionally dominated computational-linguistic research. This can be seen for example in number of morphologically complex forms belonging to one word, which in Indo-European languages is in range of ones or tens whereas for Uralic languages, it is in the range of hundreds and thousands. Furthermore, Uralic language situations share a lot of geo-political aspects: the three national languages—Finnish, Estonian and Hungarian—are comparably small languages and only moderately resourced in terms of computational-linguistics while being stable and not in threat of extinction. The recognised minority languages of western-European states, on the other hand—such as North Smi, Kven and Vro—do clearly fall in the category of lesser resourced and more threatened languages, whereas the majority of Uralic languages in the east of Europe and Siberia are close to extinction. Common to all rapid development of more advanced computational-linguistic methods is required for continued vitality of the languages in everyday life, to enable archiving and use of the languages with computers and other devices such as mobile applications.

Computational linguistic Research inside Uralistics is being carried out only in a handful of universities, research institutes and other sites and only by relatively few researchers. Our intention with organising this conference is to gather these researchers from scattered institutions together in order to share ideas and resources, and avoid duplicating efforts in gathering and enriching these scarce resources. We want to initiate more concentrated effort in collecting and improving language resources and technologies for the survival of the Uralic languages and hope that our effort today will become an ongoing tradition in the future.

For the current proceedings of The Third International Workshop on Computational Linguistics for Uralic Languages, we accepted 10 high-quality submissions about topics including computational lexicography, language documentation, optical character recognition, dependency parsing, web-as-corpus as well as automatic and rule-based morphological analysis methods. The covered languages are very broad and reach from different Smi languages, over Kven, Finnish, Komi, Udmurt, Mari, Khanty, Mansi, and Tundra Nenets. Whereas some papers describe language-specific research, others compare different languages or work on small Uralic languages in general. These contributions are all very important for the preservation and development of Uralic languages as well as for future linguistic investigations on them.

The conference was organized in collaboration with The University of Oslo St. Petersburg Representative Office and held in St. Petersburg, Russia, on January 23rd and 24th 2017. The program consisted of an invited speech by Heiki-Jaan Kaalep, a poster session, and four talks during the first day and an open discussion and individual project workshops during the second day. The current proceedings include the written versions all oral and poster presentations.

—Tommi A Pirinen, Trond Trosterud, Francis M. Tyers, Michael Rieler
Conference organisers,
January 22, 2017, St. Petersburg

Organizers:

Francis M. Tyers, UiT Norgga árktalaš universitehta
Michael Rießler, Albert-Ludwigs-Universität Freiburg
Tommi A. Pirinen, Universität Hamburg
Trond Trosterud, UiT Norgga árktalaš universitehta

Program Committee:

Eszter Simon, Magyar tudományos akadémia (Hungary)
Francis M. Tyers, UiT Norgga árktalaš universitehta (Norway)
Jack Rueter, Helsingin yliopisto (Finland)
Mans Hulden, University of Colorado at Boulder (USA)
Michael Rieler, Albert-Ludwigs-Universität Freiburg (Germany)
Miikka Silfverberg, University of Helsinki (Finland)
Tommi A. Pirinen, Universität Hanmburg (Germany)
Trond Trosterud, UiT Norgga árktalaš universitehta (Norway)
Veronika Vincze, Szegedi tudományegyetem (Hungary)
a , - Ł   (Russia)
,   ” ” (Russia)

Invited Speaker:

Heiki-Jaan Kaalep, Tartu ülikool

Table of Contents

Conference Program

Monday, January 23, 2017

10:00–10:15   Opening Remarks

10:15–11:30   Invited Talk by Heiki-Jaan Kaalep

Session 1: Poster boasters

11:30–11:33   *Synchronized Mediawiki based analyzer dictionary development*
Jack Rueter and Mika Hämäläinen

11:33–11:36   *DEMO: Giellatekno Open-source click-in-text dictionaries for bringing closely related languages into contact.*
Jack Rueter

11:36–11:39   *Languages under the influence: Building a database of Uralic languages*
Eszter Simon and Nikolett Mus

11:39–11:42   *Instant Annotations —Applying NLP Methods to the Annotation of Spoken Language Documentation Corpora*
Ciprian Gerstenberger, Niko Partanen, Michael Rießler and Joshua Wilbur

11:45–12:30   Posters and Coffee

12:30–14:00   Lunch

Session 2: Oral presentations

14:00–14:30   *Preliminary Experiments concerning Verbal Predicative Structure Extraction from a Large Finnish Corpus*
Guersande Chaminade and Thierry Poibeau

14:30–15:00   *Language technology resources and tools for Mansi: an overview*
Csilla Horváth, Norbert Szilágyi, Veronika Vincze and Ágoston Nagy

15:00–15:30   *Annotation schemes in North Sámi dependency parsing*
Francis M. Tyers and Mariya Sheyanova

15:30–16:00   *A morphological analyser for Kven*
Sindre Reino Trosterud, Trond Trosterud, Anna-Kaisa Räisänen, Leena Niiranen, Mervi Haavisto and Kaisa Maliniemi

Monday, January 23, 2017 (continued)

16:00–16:30   LRE Map, LR Matrices and LR Impact Factor

16:30–17:15   Posters, demos and coffee

17:15–18:30   ACL SIGUR business meeting

19:00–late   Conference Dinner

Tuesday, January 24, 2017

10:00–18:00   Round tables, discussions and workshopping

Synchronized Mediawiki based analyzer dictionary development

Jack Rueter
University of Helsinki
Department of Modern Languages
`jack.rueter@helsinki.fi`

Mika Hämäläinen
University of Helsinki
Department of Computer Science
`mika.hamalainen@helsinki.fi`

Abstract

Open-source analyzer dictionary development is being implemented for Skolt Sami, Ingrian, Moksha-Mordvin, etc. in the Helsinki CSC infrastructure; home of the Finnish Kielipankki 'Language Bank' and Termipankki 'Term Bank'. The proximity of minority-language corpora in need of annotation and the multiple usage of controlled wikimedia-type dictionaries make CSC an attractive site for synchronized transducer dictionary development. The open-source FST development of Uralic and other minority languages at Giellatekno-Divvun in Tromsø demonstrates a vast potential for reusage of FST-s, only augmented by open-source work in OmorFi, Apertium and Universal Dependency <http://universaldependencies.org/#language-urj>. The initial idea is to allow synchronized editing of Giellatekno XML and CSC Wiki structures via github. In addition to allowing for simple lexc LEMMA:STEM CONTINUATION_LEXICON "TRANS-LATION" ; line exports, the parallel dictionaries will provide for documentation of derivation, morpho-syntactic information on valency and government, semantics and etymology.

The 3rd International Workshop for Computational Linguistics of Uralic Languages, pages 1–7,
St. Petersburg, Russia, 23–24 January 2017. ©2017 Association for Computational Linguistics

1   Introduction

Open-source finite-state transducer development and application as we know it today in the Giellatekno infrastructure[1] at Tromsø, Norway dates back to the early 1990s. It begins with the morphological description of different Sami languages, grammatical analysis and syntax. Morphological and morphosyntactic description lays the foundation for tool building, such as Divvun[2], and working solutions attract soft coding for the application of research and tools to other languages. Open-source compilers from HFST[3] in Helsinki, are gradually worked into the infrastructure after 2008. With the growth of the research community and tool building diversity comes the practicality of reusable resources, descriptions and testing formalisms. As things improve the number of uses and users also increases. One resource, in particular, is the four-fold combination of lemma, stem, pos/continuation lexicon and gloss, afforded by many of the language projects at Giellatekno in lexc code.

Lexc code containing multiple nodes of information can be stored in XML files for xsl transformation and project-specific transducer construction. The need for multiple transducers presents itself when tagging strategies are not shared by the multiple projects of a given language. Although the two-level model may be sufficient for all projects, normative labeling, morphosyntactic information and semantic tag needs will vary for TTS, MT, ICALL, spellcheckers and other morphological analyzer projects. The Giellatekno-Divvun strategy has been to utilize one lexc and twolc in all North Sami projects with filters for selecting the necessary code. For this multiple and iterated use of resources, on the contrary, the solution presents itself in XML-format analyzer dictionaries with multiple xsl transformations and the possibility to keep up with semantic wiki strategies being adopted in open wikimedia projects[4].

At CSC in Helsinki, Finland, a sanat-server has been put into operation and provides access, initially, to the Kielipankki[5] (Finnish Language Bank) wordnet and Ludic dictionary development. The Ludic dictionary provides for Finnish-Ludic and Russian-Ludic documentation of the Ludic language in a Wikimedia environment. The Wikimedia environment is a sibling of what is used for facilitating Termipankki[6] (the Finnish Term Bank); domains and subdomains can be established for administrating access and editing rights. This type of environment is desirable for synchronic editing strategies involving XML and php input. Unlike wiktionary and wikipedia

---

[1] http://giellatekno.uit.no/

[2] http://divvun.no/

[3] http://www.ling.helsinki.fi/kieliteknologia/tutkimus/hfst/

Lene Antonsen (p.c. 2016)

[4] https://en.wiktionary.org/wiki/Wiktionary:Semantic_relations/

[5] https://www.kielipankki.fi/

[6] http://tieteentermipankki.fi/

instances, however, a wikimedia environment at CSC might be afforded better control of vital inflection-type data and allow for controlled levels of editing and citizen science.

2 XML Dictionaries

XML analyzer dictionaries initially consist of the three bare necessities for the lexc files. They contain lemma, stem and continuation class information. Additional semantic tags, as well as usage and POS information is also stored in the xml. The structure of the Skolt Sami XML dictionary at Giellatekno, in fact, goes much further but has yet to reach a level of consistency, which is due to multiple contributions from various projects. The Skolt Sami dictionary contains many fields of information and references. There are external references to audiofiles, Swadesh list instances[7] and etymological databases[8], while at the same time there are internal references to derivation, compounding, government and semantics; both ICALL and multilingual translation resources.

By integrating morphology, morphosyntax and semantics into one system, a direct link can be drawn to research dictionaries and syntactic contexts available in published fieldwork research. Utilization of research results leads of modeling XML structure after the derivation-oriented nature of research dictionaries. It directs development toward semi-automated derivation and compounding documentation. Research-language definitions (Russian, German and Finnish) provide new dimensions for tandem development of multilingual resources wherein the semantics provided by word-net mapping[9] of majority languages can be utilized in the prediction and implementation of semantic alignment in minority languages. Synchronized tandem development presupposes multi-input strategies for different projects at the single or multiple-language level, as well as an opportunity for citizen-science contribution.

At present the XML element structure contains a two-way division: one lemmaGroup <lg/> and one or more morphosyntacticGroups <mg/>. The <lg/> is associated with lemma, stem, inflection type, audio files, etymology links and derivational

---

Tommi Pirinen, p.c. 2015

[7]http://dla.library.upenn.edu/dla/olac/search.html?fq=subject_language_facet%3A"Skolt Sami"/

[8]http://kaino.kotus.fi/algu/index.php?t=etusivu&kkieli=en

In the spring of 2016, the Finno-Ugrian Society decided to make many of its early publications in fieldwork and research searchable, among other things this meant the OCR of 8 volumes of Mordvin Folklore, consisting of transcriptions with parallel German and possibly Russian translations, as well as a 2703-page dialect dictionary for the two literary languages.

[9]https://www.academia.edu/13230592/Developing_electronic_lexical_resources_for_Saami_Languages/

or compounding data. The <mg/>, however, is associated with semantics, dependencies and argument structure, as well as translations and contextual examples. There is also room for source information in many of the elements as will be noted in the sanat.csc.fi/wiki/Luokka:Sms/ entries.

3   The XML-Wiki Synchronization System and its Architecture

Because dictionary development can be done on both XML and Wiki side simultaneously, a database system is needed in between through which the latest changes on both sides can be synchronized so that the people editing the XML files have the same version as the people modifying the Mediawiki dictionary. Furthermore, data can come to the dictionary from different XML files, all of them having a slightly different structure. For instance, in the case of Skolt Sami, there are three different kinds of XML files that all need to be synchronized with the system.

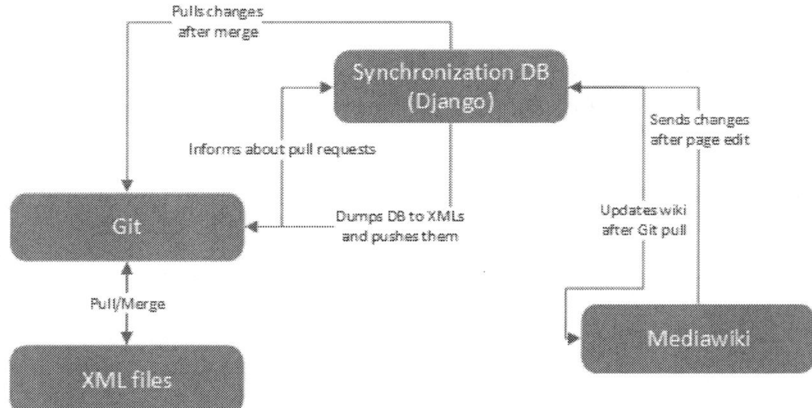

Figure 1: System architecture

The architecture of the system is described in the Figure 1. On one end, there are the XML files and the other Mediawiki. In the middle, there's a Django based service with its own Mongo based database through which the synchronization is done. Mediawiki is directly linked to the Django service, so that all the changes will be reflected to both systems directly.

A problem arising from this architecture is how conflicts are resolved. That is why only the Mediawiki side is directly linked to the Django service. The XML files need to be updated through Git. The work flow for the people working with the XML files is the following: they make modifications to the XML files in their own branches and once they are ready to release the changes to the Mediawiki side, they will create a pull request for that branch. What it means is that they want to merge their edits to the master branch which contains the production data. At this point, an automatic Travis script is executed and what it essentially does, is that it makes the Django service dump its database into XML format to the Git project, commit the possible changes and push them to the master branch. If the dictionary has been modified in the Mediawiki side, the person developing the XML files has to resolve the conflicts using Git. Because resolving conflicts is what Git is really good at, leaving the conflict resolution to that system makes our system easier to develop and maintain as we can safely assume that Git is stable enough. Once the pull request is finished and all the conflicts are resolved, the Django based system will be notified about the changes in the master branch and it will start to update its own database and Mediawiki.

Another challenge for this system is the different data structures used. XMLs have their own formatting, the Django services internal database uses Mongo which is essentially a JSON based data structure and finally Mediawiki shows its pages using its own Wiki syntax. The Django services data structure cannot be identical with the XMLs for two different reasons: first of all, even Skolt Sami has multiple different XMLs with different structures and secondly we aim to support multiple languages and make the process of integrating new languages an easy one. As a result of our architecture choice, what is mostly needed for a new language to be added to the system is an XML to/from JSON conversion script. This way we can reuse the existing Mediawiki to/from JSON conversion code, so that the Mediawiki and Django service sides can communicate with each other already when a new language with XML files is added. Thus far, this has seemed to work well when the Ingrian XML files were added to the system.

The system also needs to be easy to use for non-technical people. From people working directly with the XML files, you can expect that they know how to maintain the structure of the files, for example that every open tag has to be closed in the correct order and so on. However, from people dealing with the Mediawiki based dictionary, you cannot expect them to understand how the Wiki page needs to be structured in order for the Django service to understand it correctly. That is why when a user enters the page edit mode on Mediawiki, a form is displayed instead of the raw Wiki text. This form then turns the edits into Wiki text with Java Script so that the Mediawiki

platform can display the dictionary entry correctly. The same Java Script is used by
the Django service when it updates the pages on Mediawiki.

4   Wiki Dictionary

The Wiki-based dictionary is hosted on CSC's servers (https://sanat.csc.fi). Before this
project their Mediawiki platform already had one dictionary, Ludic, and the Finnish
WordNet. In addition to that, the Institute for the Languages in Finland (http://www.ko-
tus.fi/en) has expressed their interest in adding their own dictionaries and word lists
to the same Mediawiki platform. Since multiple parties are interested in the same
platform, it only makes sense for us to use it as well. This opens the possibility of in-
terlinking dictionaries from different providers to enhance the quality of all of them.

From the point of view of our project, the Mediawiki dictionary serves two purposes. People with editing rights can edit the dictionary easily online and other people can access an up-to-date dictionary for Uralic languages for free. The Mediawiki
infrastructure also allows for variation in the extent of editing rights. This means
that, while there are two different kinds of user groups whose needs have to be taken
into account, there is also a possibility for monitored editing by a larger and larger
contributing group of users.

For the editors, the system gives more information about each word in the page
edit mode. This includes all sorts of metadata that is useful for researchers but not so
useful for normal dictionary users. The reason why such information is not presented
to everyone is that having too much irrelevant information would only confuse the
normal dictionary users. They are probably using the dictionary to find what a certain
word means in another language and they are not so interested in, let's say, the source
from which a word came to the dictionary.

Currently, regular users are presented with lemma's part-of-speech, translation
to different languages, semantic information and etymology. In the future we would
like to include morphological transducers in the dictionary so that the user could see
with a click of a button all the possible inflections of a word. Also we would like to
link audio files and add example sentences to the entries of the dictionary.

5   Conclusions

The tandem development of analyzer dictionaries in an environment already hosting
terminology, word list and corpora resources is a challenging undertaking in itself.
Coordinating synchronized editing between multiple input infrastructures takes our

efforts to a bold extreme.

The challenge is allowing for documentation of information already available from research. We are providing for input from multiple environments, and thus rendering collaboration with a lower threshold. The establishment of a platform for direct documentation of new and old results and data means we are essentially pointing the way in future open-source work in the field.

We are finding our niche by drawing on documentational structuring from multiple language research projects and documentational needs. We recognize that our development must be available for work being done in other areas, as we will be providing an intermediate point linking transducer development, semantics, etymology and corpora annotation.

The synchronized editing interfaces, Mediawiki and XML, will bring us to a new phase in dictionary development at CSC. The presence of unanalyzed or minimally analyzed corpora for Uralic languages will provide a resource for morphosyntactic information. New methods will be applied for semiautomated integration of dictionary development and simultaneous corpora annotation.

DEMO

Giellatekno Open-source click-in-text dictionaries for bringing closely related languages into contact.

Abstract

This is a demo of online dictionaries between minority languages with open-source FST morphology and lexical work. Open-source click-in-text dictionaries, NeahttaDigiSanit (NDS), have been developed in the Giellatekno infrastructure since 2012-2013. Originally, these dictionaries were implemented to provide a Sami-language reading tool to provide click-in-text wordform recognition and translation for majority-language readers by which they could access text content written in minority languages. From the very beginning of 2013 this same dictionary has been localized not only for Sami languages, but for work with Balto-Finnic, Mordvin, Mari, Permic, Ugrian and Samoyedic languages, as well. There are now a number of NDS projects with Finnish, Hungarian, Russian and German majority langauge hubs. There are also a few instances of closely related language pairs outside of the Sami and Balto-Finnic branch; these include the Permic languages and Mordvin languages.

As of late October 2016, there are three sets of two-directional dictionaries operating between closely related languages: Udmurt<->Komi Zyrian; Komi Permyak<->Komi Zyrian, and Erzya<->Moksha.

Permic language pairs	Source	Target	Lemmas
http://kyv.oahpa.no	Udmurt	Komi Zyrian	3427
	Komi Zyrian	Udmurt	5020
	Komi Permyak	Komi Zyrian	1252
	Komi Zyrian	Komi Permyak	1981
Mordvin language pairs	Erzya	Moksha	3677
http://valks.oahpa.no	Moksha	Erzya	3613

The lemmas and their glosses have been taken from the publications by Evgeni Tsypanov (Udmurt, Komi Permyak and Komi Zyrian), and Osip Polyakov (Moksha and Erzya). Open-source FST work comes directly projects in the Giellatekno infrastructure.

Resources:
Dictionaries

О.Е. Поляков 2004: Мокшень и эрзянь кяльхнень фкакс- и аф фкаксшисна. Синь валлувкссна. Эрзянь ды мокшонь кельтнень вейкекс- ды аволь вейкексчист. Сынст валлувост. / О.Е. Поляков, J. Rueter; Н.П. Огарёвонь лемса Мордовскяй государственнай университетсь. – Саранск: «Краснай Октябрь» типографиясь. – 264 с. https://victorio.uit.no/langtech/trunk/words/dicts/mdfmyv/

The 3rd International Workshop for Computational Linguistics of Uralic Languages, pages 8–9, St. Petersburg, Russia, 23–24 January 2017. ©2017 Association for Computational Linguistics

https://victorio.uit.no/langtech/trunk/words/dicts/myvmdf/

Цыпанов, Е.А. 1999: ПЕРЫМ-КОМИ ГИЖӦД КЫВ. Сыктывкар — «Пролог» небӧг ледзанін.

https://victorio.uit.no/langtech/trunk/words/dicts/kpvkoi/
https://victorio.uit.no/langtech/trunk/words/dicts/koikpv/

Цыпанов Й. 2007: Удмурт кыввор да лыддянкуд. Россияса наукаяс академия Урал юкӧд Коми туялан шӧрин Кыв, литература да история институт. — Сыктывкар.

https://victorio.uit.no/langtech/trunk/words/dicts/udmkpv/
https://victorio.uit.no/langtech/trunk/words/dicts/kpvudm/

Open-source FSTs:

https://victorio.uit.no/langtech/trunk/langs/koi/
https://victorio.uit.no/langtech/trunk/langs/kpv/
https://victorio.uit.no/langtech/trunk/langs/mdf/
https://victorio.uit.no/langtech/trunk/langs/myv/
https://victorio.uit.no/langtech/trunk/langs/udm/

Languages under the influence:
Building a database of Uralic languages

Eszter Simon, Nikolett Mus
Research Institute for Linguistics
Hungarian Academy of Sciences
{simon.eszter, mus.nikolett}@nytud.mta.hu

Abstract

For most of the Uralic languages, there is a lack of systematically collected, consequently transcribed and morphologically annotated text corpora. This paper sums up the steps, the preliminary results and the future directions of building a linguistic corpus of some Uralic languages, namely Tundra Nenets, Udmurt, Synya Khanty, and Surgut Khanty. The experiences of building a corpus containing both old and modern, and written and oral data samples are discussed. Principles concerning data collection strategies of languages with different level of vitality and endangerment are discussed. Methodologies and challenges of data processing, and the levels of linguistic annotation are also described in detail.

1   Introduction

This paper sums up the steps, the preliminary results and the future directions of building a linguistic corpus of some Uralic languages within the research project called *Languages under the Influence*. The project started in February 2016 and lasts until July 2017 and is funded by the Hungarian National Research, Development and Innovation Office (grant ID: ERC_HU_15 118079).

It is a pre-ERC project getting national support to enter the European Research Council (ERC) programme[1], thus it is a pilot project. Its aim is to create the theoretical

[1]https://erc.europa.eu/

The 3rd International Workshop for Computational Linguistics of Uralic Languages, pages 10–24,
St. Petersburg, Russia, 23–24 January 2017. ©2017 Association for Computational Linguistics

and methodological basis of an ERC project proposal, which is called as 'the main project' in the article.

The main project has a twofold objective. As for the theoretical investigations, it focuses on potential syntactic changes affected by the heavy influence of the Russian language in several Uralic languages spoken in the Russian Federation (mainly in Siberia). Our research covers, among others, the change of basic word order (i.e. the SOV-to-SVO order), the spreading of finite subordination and clause-initial complementizers, and the diversification of indefinite pronouns. The languages involved are *Tundra Nenets, Udmurt, Synya Khanty*, and *Surgut Khanty*.

On the other hand, the main project's computational objective is to build a linguistically annotated database of written and spoken sources in the aforementioned languages, which makes it possible to research on Uralic–Russian language contacts. In order to observe syntactic changes of minority languages under the influence, we aim at processing texts collected from different times. It is known, however, that the literacy of Uralic languages do not have a long history and tradition. The oldest sources included in our project originate from the beginning of the 20th century (when organized expeditions were undertaken in order to document and describe Uralic languages). In addition, we gather data from published and/or electronically accessible sources, which are presented by fieldworks undertaken recently. We focus on selecting texts provided by as many authors as possible from different social classes, age, sex, dialects and genres. Furthermore, our activities will include fieldwork, during which we will collect contemporary spoken language material, thus the database will represent the written and the spoken versions of the languages as well.

Within the pilot project, text samples from the two time periods for all the aforementioned languages have been collected and partly processed and annotated. In this paper, we discuss considerations taken into account and methods used in the pilot corpus building process, which indeed will be applied in the main project as well. The structure of the remaining part of the article is as follows: In Section 2, we discuss the main principal criteria behind corpus building. Section 3 describes the collected text material and the problems we face with when aiming at creating such a corpus. The text processing steps are detailed in Section 4, while Section 5 presents the structure of the corpus. We conclude in Section 6, which contains the future directions as well.

2   Theoretical considerations

We follow several principal criteria within the pilot project which form the basis even of the whole corpus building process of the main project. Since the Uralic languages dealt with are endangered and/or poorly documented, we think that creating a database which follows the basic concepts of language documentation is of huge importance, as detailed in 2.1. Other principal criteria are: following international standards on every level of corpus building (2.2), consistency which would apply on all levels (2.3), and using and creating freely available resources (2.4).

2.1 Language documentation

One of the principal criteria of the pilot project is following some basic principles of language documentation (cf. [1, 2]). First, we focus on compiling *primary data* in Himmelmann's sense [3], i.e. we collected data types that were produced at a specific point in time and space by a specific speaker instead of collecting and using generalized secondary data, e.g. elicited data (that may be corrupted). This rule is also applied to our fieldwork(s), during which we prefer to document the languages in their natural forms, i.e. to record language variants that are not influenced by the style of genres (as in the case of folklore texts), or by some prescriptive considerations (as in the case of journalism). The application of this principle led us to the second concept, i.e. collecting and storing the *context* of the data (metadata), which generally concerns the recording time and place, the age, gender and spoken dialects of the informants. The collection of metadata is also needed for other scientific fields, e.g. for sociolinguistics, anthropology, and sociology [4]. Third, we aim at building a database whose content is *transferable* both in linguistic and in technical terms. Consequently, both the representation, i.e. the transcription, and the analysis, i.e. the morphological tags, of our data is not restricted to any theory or method. Finally, we make our data *available* for further theoretical and applied research, as well as for direct use by the relevant language communities.

However, certain rules and conditions of language documentation are necessarily contravened in our project. For instance, as languages are still most typically used in speech, collecting spoken data has primacy in language documentation. This principle, however, has its limits in the case of the historical data, such as the availability of the original sound recordings. Therefore, we decided to collect old texts that appeared in critical editions instead of inscriptions or original manuscripts. Although these editions usually contain smaller range of text genre, they still provide rich metadata and useful information about the rules followed during the transcription of spoken data. In the case of contemporary written language samples, we aim for selecting texts which are provided by as many authors as possible from different social classes, age, gender, dialects and genres. As our project has its time limit, we need to break the rule of collecting full range of textual genres and registers and primarily focus on those ones which may typically show the results of a potential language contact. These written genres are usually the types which are closer to the spoken language, such as blogs and tweets, see more details in Section 3. Finally, the written language varieties of the languages concerned are typically produced by only a few writers, therefore, the sociolinguistical parameters may not be balanced in our corpus.

2.2 International standards

Another criterium is following international standards on every level of the corpus building process. Therefore, we only use standard Unicode characters, we provide phonemic transcription using the letters of the International Phonetic Alphabet (IPA), we follow the Leipzig Glossing Rules (LGR)[2] and abbreviations, and we use standard file formats, as detailed below.

The Unicode Standard[3] is a multilingual coding system which provides a consistent encoding for most of the world's writing systems. Recently, it became an international standard, which supports the worldwide interchange, processing and display of written texts of diverse languages. One of the great advantages of Unicode is that it properly handles various accented and multi-accented characters, since basic characters and combining diacritical marks are represented by their own codes. Unicode also contains all of the Cyrillic characters used in the orthographies of the aforementioned languages. Moreover, the Unicode Consortium provides new supplements in each release for users to be able to handle and represent the proper characters used by minority communities. For example, the characters Ԏ (U+052E Cyrillic capital letter el with descender) and ԏ (U+052F Cyrillic small letter el with descender) were released in version 7.0 in 2014 based on the character request proposal submitted to the Unicode Technical Committee by Tapani Salminen[4]. Salminen provides evidence from recent native publications that these characters are needed, since a descender is used in common typographic practice of the Northern Khanty, Eastern Khanty, Tundra Nenets and Forest Nenets languages. Before version 7.0, replacement characters were used instead of them, mostly Ԓ (U+0512 Cyrillic capital letter el with hook) and ԓ (U+0513 Cyrillic small letter el with hook) or Ӆ (U+04C5 Cyrillic capital letter el with tail) and ӆ (U+04C6 Cyrillic small letter el with tail), but since then the proper characters be can used.

The Unicode code charts also contain all of the widely used IPA characters, thus every textual element (Uralic transcriptions, IPA transliteration, Cyrillic characters) can be stored with standard Unicode characters, which makes it possible to replace the old, makeshift font collections and to follow the international standards.

---

[2] https://www.eva.mpg.de/lingua/pdf/Glossing-Rules.pdf
[3] http://unicode.org/
[4] http://www.unicode.org/L2/L2012/12052-khanty-nenets.pdf

Language documenters of the languages concerned in this project used different subtypes of the traditional Finno-Ugric transcription (FUT) system (see details in Section 4.2). However, these Latin-based transcription systems are not standardized nor unified, even within one language. For this reason, it is important to publish the texts using the IPA system, as it makes the texts readable for further areas of linguistics outside Uralistics.

On the morphological annotation level, we follow the Leipzig Glossing Rules with some modifications. The tokens and the corresponding pieces of morphological information are aligned, i.e. the following annotations are added to each token of the corpus: lemma, part-of-speech (POS) tag, morphological labels of derivational and inflectional categories, and English translation of the lemma. The glosses are converted from the output of a morphological analyzer developed for the language concerned. As a consequence, if the output is not segmented on the level of morphemes, even the glosses will not contain morpheme-by-morpheme correspondence. In the case if the morphological analyzer is able to produce morpheme-level segmentation, segmentable morphemes will be separated by hyphens according to the second rule of the LGR.

The LGR also contains a proposed list of category labels which were applied for our corpus. Since this list does not cover all morphological phenomena existing in the examined Uralic languages, two further tagsets were used to supplement the original list of the LGR. One of them is the Wikipedia page of the list of glossing abbreviations[5] which provides a more detailed list of grammatical terms and their abbreviations for interlinear glossing. The other source was the collection of abbreviation lists provided by the reference grammars of the languages in question. When choosing our tags, we preferred the standard category terms and labels over the particular ones.

We follow international standards even in the file formats. All text files are UTF-8 encoded plain text files. The token-level annotations are represented in separate columns of `tsv` files, which can be easily converted into XML files or can be directly imported into ELAN as tiers. For transcribing and archiving audio and video data, we use ELAN which is one of the most widely used multimedia annotation tool[6]. ELAN allows audio and video recordings to be time-aligned with multilayered annotations, called tiers. The linguistic annotations and the metadata are stored in a hierarchical structure, which can be exported as standard XML files, which can be used as an input of further text processing steps.

---

[5] https://en.wikipedia.org/wiki/List_of_glossing_abbreviations
[6] http://tla.mpi.nl/tools/tla-tools/elan/

2.3 Consistency

Consistency is the third principal criterium which would apply on all levels: a unified character table has been created to be able to ask one query to the whole corpus; and similarly, the same morphological label is used for the same morphological phenomenon.

Research in language documentation aims at creating long lasting, multipurpose and multifaceted databases in which language technology can definitely help to create systematically annotated corpora, rather than eclectic data collections. The main difference between the former and the latter one is consistency.

Consistency is a basic requirement so that one can ask a query on the whole corpus. One of the great advantages of corpora is that they provide not only separate examples but all instances of the searched term, so analyses based on frequency become available. This important property of corpora can be ensured only if one follows the principle of consistency, and always uses the same appropriate character for representing the same letter and different characters for representing different letters. Therefore, we created a unified character table which contains all possibly used characters in all writing, transliteration and transcription systems of all languages concerned.

As for the level of morphology, the glosses are converted from the output of several morphological analyzers, thus a mapping of the different tags into the set of the unified labels has to be conducted. As a consequence, one morphological phenomenon is always signed with one and the same label.

2.4 Open access

During the whole corpus building process, we aim for following the philosophy of open access, which has two aspects. First, we prefer to use freely available language processing tools and to re-use already collected data sets if it is possible. Second, the results of the project (text and processing resources) will also be freely available.

We plan to make the database available, not only as a downloadable version, but also via an online search interface, which offers the user several features that greatly facilitate the linguistic analysis of large amounts of authentic linguistic data. Moreover, considering the need for long-term preservation in order to assure that these data will be available for future generations, we want to provide the structured data for an international language archive which offers archiving service, such as the Documentation of Endangered Languages (DOBES) corpus hosted by The Language Archive.

3   Text collection and sampling

As mentioned before, the goal of the text selection is to design a corpus that contains reliable, natural, and representative data. There are many factors, however, that one has to consider with respect to the selected Uralic languages when collecting text material. The two main factors discussed here are (i) the level of endangerment of the languages and (ii) the difficulties of data sampling.

Both the vitality and the documentational status vary considerably between the languages of our project. The variation is remarkable especially between the Udmurt language and the languages spoken in Siberia, i.e. Synya Khanty, Surgut Khanty and Tundra Nenets.

The EGIDS level[7] of Udmurt is 5, i.e. it is *developing*, which means that there is literature which is available in a standardized form, though it is not yet widespread or sustainable. In the case of the other three Siberian languages, this value is 6b, i.e. *threatened*, which means that the use of the languages is restricted to the domains of home and family interactions. Native speakers typically belong to the older generation, while the younger ones are losing their heritage languages. Despite the fact that the speaking communities of the three languages in Siberia have territorial autonomies, they are not considered as official languages in the Russian Federation. On the contrary, Udmurt is one of the official languages of Udmurtia. As the languages spoken in Siberia are considered to be of low prestige, efforts of language planning and language revitalization have only sporadically be made in the area. Similarly to several indigenous languages found in Siberia, they are regarded as poorly described and documented languages.

The difference between the levels of vitality results in the limitation or lack of availability of certain text types in the case of the languages spoken in Siberia. While there is a relatively large amount of printed text material collected from speakers who can be characterized as being "old, fluent speakers" of the community (cf. [5]), there is no data from the informal text genres such as blogs or tweets produced by the younger generation. Although several fieldtrips have been undertaken to the traditional territories recently, the collected texts are usually published only in a printed form, or if electronically, they are not available for the research community. If there are electronic corpora or text collections available, they do not provide a representative sample of the language.

Consequently, in the case of the old texts, we selected those folklore texts that were collected in the beginning of the 20th century and (mainly) edited by the fieldworkers themselves. The old Synya Khanty texts come from the collection of Wolfgang Steinitz

---

[7] https://www.ethnologue.com/about/language-status

[6], which was published in 1975 but collected in the 30s. The old Surgut Khanty texts were collected by Heikki Paasonen [7] in 1900–01 at the Yugan river. As for Udmurt, old text material comes from two sources: once, from the collection of Bernát Munkácsi [8] from 1887, and second, from the collection of Yrjö Wichmann [9] which was published in 1901. The old Tundra Nenets texts are also folklore texts, collected by Toivo Lehtisalo [10] in 1911–12. Even though the genre of these text samples is the same, we tried to keep the ratio of the (sub)dialects, the age and the gender of the informants as balanced as possible. The full table with metadata is available on the web site of the project (the URL will only be provided in the camera ready version).

The sources of the new text material are more diverse. In the case of these texts, we aim to collect and process texts from genres that may potentially represent Russian contact. For this purpose, blogs, interviews appeared in newspapers or in books, and narratives of personal stories have been found suitable. The new Khanty data contains transcribed interviews recently collected during fieldwork. The new Udmurt texts were sampled from the blogs called *Мынам малпанъёсы*[8] and *Марайко*[9]. The new Tundra Nenets data contains interviews from the newspaper entitled *Нярьяна Нгэрм* ('Red North') published in Salekhard. Besides, we acquired and preprocessed several recently collected folklore text samples from the collection of Labanauskas [11] and Pushkareva–Khomich [12]. For each type of new text/data, we clarify their access rights and apply for authorisation.

The new spoken data mainly originate from fieldwork of our project members. These data will be transcribed and time-aligned in ELAN. We plan to collect contemporary data from the same territories from where the old data samples originate, with which we aim at reducing the effects of the influence factors.

4   Text processing

The first step of the corpus building workflow is the acquisition of source data, which typically contains the steps of scanning and OCRing or downloading from the web, see Section 4.1. The language documenters used Latin-based transcription systems, while the languages concerned use Cyrillic writing systems, and we aim at creating the IPA transliteration for the text samples in all languages, therefore we have to deal with several transcriptions and transliterations, see for details in Section 4.2. The morphological analysis and disambiguation is discussed in Section 4.3.

---

[8] `http://udmurto4ka.blogspot.hu/`
[9] `http://marjamoll.blogspot.hu/`

4.1 Acquisition of the original text material

A significant part of the linguistic material was only available in print. In this case, digitization was carried out by scanning followed by a conversion process from the scanned images into regular text files aided by an OCR software.

Since we work with several writing, transcription and transliteration systems, a key aspect of an OCR software was its ability to be trained. For this purpose, we used the Abbyy FineReader Professional edition[10], which can be trained in an interactive way and produces a fairly good quality result.

Some new text samples were acquired by downloading them from the web. In these cases, the plain text had to be extracted from HTML sources or PDF files. Because of the diverse sources, a kind of character-level normalization is needed. For this purpose, a `Perl` script is used which lists all of the Unicode characters used in the document. Based on this, foreign language parts and not properly used characters can be removed or changed, such as in the case of the Cyrillic letter el with descender, see Section 2.2.

4.2 Transcription and transliteration

The database contains each text material at least in its original transcription used by the language documenter and in IPA transliteration. Moreover, since the writing system of the languages concerned is based on the Cyrillic alphabet, we preserve the original Cyrillic script, if it is available. If not, we create it in a conversion step, if it is needed for the morphological analysis. Since some morphological analyzers only accepts the input in a given FUT transcription, texts in some languages had to be converted into that transcription as well.

The Finno-Ugric transcription (FUT) system or the Uralic Phonetic Alphabet is a phonetic transcription system first published by Eemil Nestor Setälä [13] and only used in the field of Uralistics. It is called one system, however, it is actually a common name for several transcription systems developed and used by researchers and language documenters in the Uralic studies from the end of the 19th century until recently.

The systems of Wolfgang Steinitz, Márta Csepregi [14], Bernát Munkácsi, Yrjö Wichmann, Toivo Lehtisalo and Péter Hajdú [15] differ from each other very much. Each of them follow his/her own inner logic, which is sometimes hard to be detected, additionally they are not consequent in the sense that they frequently apply different characters for the same sound and vice versa. For example, in the case of

---

[10]`http://finereader.abbyy.com/`

Surgut Khanty, the close central rounded vowel represented with the IPA symbol /ʉ/ is marked with /ü/ by Steinitz and with /ŭ/ by Márta Csepregi.

There are altogether 11 conversion directions for the four languages, as detailed below. The old Synya Khanty texts are originally transcribed by Steinitz, who used his own FUT-like system, which has been converted first into IPA, and second into another FUT-like transcription used by the developers of the morphological analyzer for Synya Khanty (see later in Section 4.3).

The old Surgut Khanty texts were kindly provided us by Elena Skribnik and Zsófia Schön, members of the Ob-Ugric Database (OUDB) research project[11]. The OUDB text corpus contains the texts only in IPA transliteration, thus the Paasonen texts are available only in IPA. However, the modern Surgut Khanty texts are written with Cyrillic characters, which have been converted first into the transcription system of Márta Csepregi, then from that into IPA.

As for the Udmurt language, we had to create conversion rules for four directions. Once, we compiled the conversion rules from the transcription of Bernát Munkácsi and Yrjö Wichmann into IPA. Since the available morphological analyzers for Udmurt (see Section 4.3) only accept Cyrillic script, we had to create the transliteration rules for the direction from IPA to Cyrillic. In the case of modern Udmurt texts, the inverse direction is used, since we have to create the IPA transliteration of texts written in Cyrillic as well.

The old Tundra Nenets texts transcribed by Lehtisalo are exceptions in the sense, that they were OCRed directly in the transcription system of Péter Hajdú, not in that of Lehtisalo. The reason behind this is that Lehtisalo's transcription is unduly difficult, and a part of the characters could not be represented by standard Unicode characters. Therefore, the starting point of the conversion was the Hajdú transcription which was converted into IPA and then into Cyrillic, the latter one for being the input of the morphological analyzer. And last but not least, the modern Cyrillic Tundra Nenets texts are also converted into IPA.

First, manually compiled transcription rules were created for all directions by linguist experts of the languages concerned. These rules were then transformed into substitution commands expressed by extended regular expressions which can be fed to the Unix command sed with the option -f. Thus, it is a typical rule-based system, one of whose shortcomings is that it is language-dependent, i.e. the system is not portable to other languages or to other directions without changing. Since the rules must be ordered, it can be quite difficult to incorporate new rules into the system. Moreover, it is hard to keep track of all rules and a single error may cause the system to malfunction. However, rule-based systems have advantages as well, namely

---

[11] http://www.oudb.gwi.uni-muenchen.de/

the high precision they achieve. Since all of the converted texts are checked and corrected by linguist experts, we rather vote for higher precision, even at the cost of difficulty.

During the process of the transcriptions one barrier arose which is resulted from the lack of the standard spelling of the old and modern texts. In both cases, we avoided to standardize the different forms that appeared in the texts even when they apparently represented the same word. We decided to keep these "inconsistent" forms, because the standardizing process may easily lead to the loss of important information regarding the phonetic system of the languages.

4.3   Morphological analysis

The corpus will contain rich linguistic annotation even on the morphological level. For each token, its lemma, its POS tag and its English gloss will be added as annotations. As mentioned in Section 2.2, the morphological annotations will be carried out by the application of the available morphological analyzers, by the conversion of glosses from their output, and by the manual correction of the output of the conversion. Therefore, if the morphological analyzer is capable to create morpheme-by-morpheme segmentation, the tokens will also be morph-level segmented.

There are existing morphological analyzers for three of the four languages concerned, with which the process of the morphological annotation can be supported, however the whole annotation process cannot be conducted fully automatically.

The most well-known text processing framework for under-resourced Uralic languages is Giellatekno[12]. It provides a fully established framework for creating language processing tools, such as proofing tools, digital dictionaries and morphological analyzers. The latter one has been developed for Udmurt, Northern Khanty and Tundra Nenets.

Besides, there are morphological tools developed for small Uralic languages, such as Udmurt and Synya Khanty, by a Hungarian language technology company (MorphoLogic) and the Research Institute for Linguistics of the Hungarian Academy of Sciences [16]. These analyzers are not open source tools, but they are available via an online interface[13]. They output an HTML file containing all potential analyses of each token. To support the process of manual checking and disambiguation, we use a web-based interface which was originally created for the disambiguation of Old Hungarian texts [17]. The proper analysis can be chosen from a pop-up menu containing a list of possible analyses which appears when the mouse cursor is placed over the

---

[12]http://giellatekno.uit.no/
[13]http://www.morphologic.hu/urali/

word. The analyses provided by the Giellatekno analyzers are also converted so that
to be fed to this web-based interface.

For the Synya Khanty texts, we use the analyzer of MorphoLogic. Its reason is
that the Giellatekno analyzer needs Cyrillic input, while all of our sources are in some
Latin-based transcriptions.

As far as we know, the Surgut Khanty language is the only one of the four languages we deal with for which there is no morphological analyzer. Based on Zipf's
law, the large part of the text is covered by the most frequent words, thus if we provide
the gloss for the first n most frequent words from a lookup, the pains of the manual
work can be highly reduced. For this reason, a linguist expert created a table with
the morphological codes and the English translation of the lemma for the 122 most
frequent words of the modern texts, from which the glosses for the 64% of the text
can be automatically generated.

For the morphological analysis of the Udmurt texts, we use the analyzer of MorphoLogic, since it provides morph-level segmentation and Hungarian translation as
well.

In the case of Tundra Nenets, we use the Giellatekno analyzer. However, the
grammar files in Giellatekno describe another dialect and follow another grammar.
For this reason, we plan to create new grammar files for Tundra Nenets within the
framework of Giellatekno, which may be used for morphological analysis of this dialect of Tundra Nenets according to the grammar of Nikolaeva [18] in the future.

5   The structure of the corpus

The corpus has three main annotation levels, each of which has an obligatory version
which must be created for each text sample. Two annotation levels are token-level
aligned, while one is sentence-level aligned. The first level is the level of the original
text itself, which can be written either in Cyrillic or in a FUT transcription, but it must
have an IPA transliteration, which is the obligatory version at this level. Token-level
alignment means in this case that several transcriptions and transliterations of each
token can be seen side-by-side in the tsv files. The morphological annotation for each
token contains the lemma, the POS tag and the English gloss. The third annotation
level is the level of translations, where the obligatory translation is the English one,
however there are several text samples which have German, Hungarian or Russian
translation as well. The different language translations are sentence-level aligned.

The token- and sentence-level aligned text samples will be imported into ELAN,
where spoken data will also be sentence-level time-aligned. ELAN presents the annotation levels as horizontal tiers, which is illustrated by the Tundra Nenets example

YRK Hajdú:	jā	mīdaxana	amkerta	jaŋkūwi
YRK IPA:	ja	mi:daxana	ămkerta	jăŋkuwi
YRK Cyrillic:	я	мыдахана	амкэрта	яңкувы
lemma:	я	мы	ңамгэ	яңгось
POS:	N	Ptcp	Pron.neg	V
gloss:	earth	create.IPFV.PTCP.LOC	something.CONC	neg.EX.INFER.3SG

ENG:	when the earth was created, there was nothing
GER:	zur zeit der erschaffung der erde gab es nichts
HUN:	a Föld teremtésének idején nem volt semmi

Table 1: Token- and sentence-level aligned text sample in Tundra Nenets.

in Table 1.

6 Conclusion and future work

This paper discussed the most important theoretical considerations and the process of building a linguistically annotated database of certain endangered Uralic languages within the framework of the research project called *Languages under the Influence*. The general theoretical considerations applied in our work cover the main principles of language documentation, the use of international standards, the principle of consistency and open access. We addressed problems of collecting text samples in endangered languages and provided solution to resolve these specific problems.

Our database contain token- and sentence-level aligned data for four languages: Tundra Nenets, Udmurt, Synya Khanty and Surgut Khanty. Each text sample is available in at least in IPA transliteration, extended with morphological information and with English translation. The still under construction thus ever growing database is freely available via the URL of our web site which will be provided in the camera ready version of the paper.

Since it is an ongoing project, several future directions emerge during each corpus building step. We aim for creating a fully annotated database containing at least 4000 tokens text samples from the two time period for all the aforementioned languages until the end of the pilot project. Long-term future plans highly depend on the result of the ERC project proposal.

As mentioned, all results of the pilot project will be freely available. Not only the converted, translated and morphologically annotated text samples are freely available, but we will provide all conversion rules and tools as well as the table of the unified morphological tagset with the unified character table. We also plan to develop an online search interface which offers several features.

Acknowledgments

The research presented in this article has been funded by the Hungarian National Research, Development and Innovation Office (grant ID: ERC_HU_15 118079).

Database building is a group effort; beside the authors, the following researchers have been contributing to it: Erika Asztalos, Katalin Gugán, Ágnes Kalivoda, Nóra Lien Nguyen-Dang, Eszter Ruttkay-Miklián, Orsolya Tánczos.

Our thanks go to: Zsófia Schön who helped us in the conversion of modern Surgut Khanty texts; Elena Skribnik and Zsófia Schön for kindly providing us the glossed texts of Paasonen; A. S. Pesikova and A. N. Volkova who gave us permission to use their interview transcriptions.

References

[1] Peter K. Austin. Language documentation in the 21st century. *JournaLIPP*, (3):57–71, 2014.

[2] Anthony C. Woodbury. Language documentation. In Julia Austin, Peter K.; Sallabank, editor, *The Cambridge Handbook of Endangered Languages*, pages 159–186. Cambridge University Press, 2011.

[3] Nikolaus P. Himmelmann. Linguistic data types and the interface between language documentation and description. *Language Documentation and Conservation*, 6:187–207, 2012.

[4] Rogier Blokland, Marina Fedina, Ciprian Gerstenberger, Niko Partanen, Michael Rießler, and Joshua Wilbur. Language documentation meets language technology. In *First International Workshop on Computational Linguistics for Uralic Languages*, number 2 in Septentrio Conference Series, pages 8–18, 2015.

[5] Colette Grinevald and Michel Bert. Speakers and communities. In Julia Austin, Peter K.; Sallabank, editor, *The Cambridge Handbook of Endangered Languages*, pages 45–65. Cambridge University Press, 2011.

[6] Wolfgang Steinitz. *Ostjakologische Arbeiten*. Akadémiai Kiadó, Budapest, 1975.

[7] Edith Vértes, editor. *Heikki Paasonens surgutostjakische Textsammlungen am Jugan. Neu transkribiert, bearbeitet, übersetzt und mit Kommentaren versehen von Edith Vértes*, volume 240 of *Mémoires de la Société Finno-Ougrienne*. Suomalais-Ugrilainen Seura, Helsinki, 2001.

[8] Bernát Munkácsi. *Votják népköltészeti hagyományok*. Magyar Tudományos Akadémia, Budapest, 1887.

[9] Yrjö Wichmann. *Wotjakische Sprachproben II. Sprichwörter, Rätsel, Märchen, Sagen und Erzählungen*. Helsinki, 1901.

[10] Toivo Lehtisalo. *Juraksamojedische Volksdichtung*. Suomalais-Ugrilainen Seura, Helsinki, 1947.

[11] К. И. Лабанаускас. *Ненецкий фольклор. Мифы, сказки, исторические предания. Вып. 5*. Красноярск, 1995.

[12] Е. Т. Пушкарёва and Л. В. Хомич. *Фольклор ненцев*. Новосибирск, 2001.

[13] Eemil Nestor Setälä. Über transskription der finnisch-ugrischen sprachen. *Finnisch-ugrische Forschungen*, 1:15–52, 1901.

[14] Márta Csepregi. *Szurguti osztják chrestomathia*. Szeged, 2011.

[15] Péter Hajdú. *Chrestomathia Samoiedica*. Tankönyvkiadó, Budapest, 1989.

[16] Attila Novák. Morphological Tools for Six Small Uralic Languages. In *Proceedings of the Fifth International Conference on Language Resources and Evaluation (LREC'06)*, pages 925–930. ELRA.

[17] Attila Novák, György Orosz, and Nóra Wenszky. Morphological annotation of Old and Middle Hungarian corpora. In *Proceedings of the 7th Workshop on Language Technology for Cultural Heritage, Social Sciences, and Humanities*, pages 43–48, Sofia, Bulgaria, August 2013. Association for Computational Linguistics.

[18] Irina Nikolaeva. *A Grammar of Tundra Nenets*. Mouton de Gruyter, 2014.

Instant Annotations – Applying NLP Methods to the Annotation of Spoken Language Documentation Corpora

Ciprian Gerstenberger[*]
University of Tromsø – The Arctic University of Norway
Giellatekno – Saami Language Technology
ciprian.gerstenberger@uit.no

Niko Partanen
University of Hamburg / University of Freiburg
Department of Uralic Studies / Department of Scandinavian Studies
niko.partanen@uni-hamburg.de

Michael Rießler[†]
ENS & PSL Research University / University of Freiburg
LaTTiCe / Department of Scandinavian Studies
michael.riessler@skandinavistik.uni-freiburg.de

Joshua Wilbur
University of Freiburg
Department of Scandinavian Studies
joshua.wilbur@skandinavistik.uni-freiburg.de

[*]The order of the names of the authors is alphabetical.

[†]Michael Rießler's contribution to this work has received support of TransferS (laboratoire d'excellence, program "Investissements d'avenir" ANR-10-IDEX-0001-02 PSL* and ANR-10-LABX-0099).

The 3rd International Workshop for Computational Linguistics of Uralic Languages, pages 25–36,
St. Petersburg, Russia, 23–24 January 2017. ©2017 Association for Computational Linguistics

Abstract

The paper describes work-in-progress by the Pite Saami, Kola Saami and Izhva Komi language documentation projects, all of which use similar data and technical frameworks and are carried out in Freiburg and in collaboration with Hamburg, Syktyvkar, Tromsø and Uppsala. Our projects work in the endangered language documentation framework and record new spoken language data, digitize available recordings and annotate these multimedia data in order to provide comprehensive language corpora as databases for future research *on* and *for* endangered and under-described Uralic speech communities. Applying NLP methods in language documentation – specifically rule-based morphological and syntactic analyzers – helps us to create more systematically annotated corpora, rather than eclectic data collections. We propose a step-by-step approach to reach higher-level annotations by using and improving truly computational methods. Ultimately, the spoken corpora created by our projects will be useful for scientifically significant quantitative investigations on these languages in the future.

1   Introduction

Endangered language documentation (aka documentary linguistics) aims at the provision of long-lasting, comprehensive, multifaceted and multipurpose records of linguistic practices characteristic of a given speech community [1, 2, 3, 4]. The field has made huge technological progress in regard to collaborative tools and user interfaces for transcribing, searching, and archiving multimedia recordings. However, paradoxically, the field has only rarely considered applying NLP methods to more efficiently annotate qualitatively and quantitatively significant corpora. This is despite the fact that the relevant computational methods and tools are well-known from corpus-driven linguistic research on larger written languages and are even applied to spoken varieties of these languages.

Although relatively small endangered languages are increasingly in the focus of computational linguistic research (see especially Giellatekno for Northern Saami [5] and other languages, a different approach is [6]), these projects work predominantly with *written* language varieties. Current computational linguistic projects on endangered languages seem to have simply copied their approach from already established research on the major languages, including the focus on written language. The resulting corpora are impressively large for these minority languages and include higher-level morphosyntactic annotations. However, they represent a limited range of text genres, typically including formal styles, and they include large portion of translations from the relevant majority languages.[1]

---

[1] The metadata provided with the Northern Saami written corpus at Giellatekno [7] suggests that the

On the other hand, researchers working in the framework of endangered language documentation (so-called "documentary linguistics"), i.e. fieldwork-based documentation, preservation, and description of endangered languages, often collect and annotate natural texts from a variety of spoken genres and including formal and informal styles. Commonly, the resulting spoken language corpora have phonemic transcriptions as well as several morphosyntactic annotation layers produced either manually or semi-manually with the help of software like Field Linguist's Toolbox (or Toolbox, for short),[2] FieldWorks Language Explorer (or FLEx, for short)[3] or similar tools. Common morphosyntactic annotations include glossed text with morpheme-by-morpheme interlinearization. Whereas these annotations are qualitatively rich, including the time alignment of annotation layers to the original audio/video recordings, the resulting corpora are relatively small and rarely reach 150,000 word tokens. Two examples of comparably large corpora created in this approach and supposedly even exceeding the number of 150,000 tokens, are the Nganasan corpus described by [9][4] and the corpus of Forest and Tundra Enets [10].[5] Typically, such spoken corpora are smaller, as is the case for the annotated corpus of spoken Beserman Udmurt comprising 65,000 tokens[6], the annotated corpora of spoken Eastern Khanty and Southern Selkup [11],[7] and the annotated corpora of Tundra Nenets and Northern Khanty.[8] The main reason for the limited size of such annotated language documentation corpora is that (semi-)manual glossing is an extremely time consuming task.

Another problem we identify especially in the documentation of small Uralic languages is that projects sometimes ignore the existence of orthographies and prefer phonemic transcription. Examples for recent projects which use phonemic transcription instead of an orthographic standard are the Khanty, Tundra Nenets, and Udmurt documentations described by [12] (in the current proceedings), the Northern Selkup documentation currently carried out as part of the INEL project,[9] as well as the corpora mentioned in the preceding paragraph. Note that most Uralic languages (or at

---

portion of non-translated texts is rather high, which would be against our earlier statement in [8].

[2] `http://www-01.sil.org/computing/toolbox/`

[3] `http://fieldworks.sil.org/flex/`

[4] Inferred from [9], who do not quantify the corpus in terms of tokens but mention the inclusion of "59 texts", and the description of somehow related data at `http://www.iling-ran.ru/gusev/Nganasan/`, mentioning "14,928 sentences (including approximately 28,000 types)" [our translation].

[5] Olesya Khanina, p.c.

[6] `http://urn.fi/urn:nbn:fi:lb-2015081401`

[7] An indication of the actual size, in terms of texts, sentences tokens or the like, is not given.

[8] `http://larkpie.net/siberianlanguages/recordings/tundra-nenets/` and `http://larkpie.net/siberianlanguages/northern-khanty/`; an indication of the actual size, in terms of texts, sentences tokens or the like, is not given.

[9] `https://inel.corpora.uni-hamburg.de/?page_id=173`; according to the INEL project application, which was co-authored by one of the current authors; a general introduction to INEL is [13].

least their main variants) have established written standards as the result of institutionalized and/or community-driven language planning and revitalization efforts. For some of these languages, e.g. Northern-Khanty, Komi-Zyrian, Northern Selkup, Tundra Nenets or Udmurt, a significant amount of printed texts can be found in books and newspapers[10] and several of these languages are also used digitally on the Internet today.[11] Last but not least, there are at least small dictionaries available for all of these languages, several of which have already been digitized. The use of materials like these in automatic corpus annotation has already been reported as a well working approach [15].

Particularly when basic phonological and morphological descriptions are already available and can serve as a resource for accessing phonological and morphological structures (which is arguably true for the majority of Uralic languages), we question the special value given to time-consuming phonemic transcriptions and (semi-)manual morpheme-by-morpheme interlinearization. Instead, we propose a step-by-step approach to reach higher-level annotations by using and improving truly computational methods, while systematically integrating all available textual, lexicographic, and grammatical resources into the language documentation endeavor (see also [8]).

We suggest the following two main principles, which we have begun implementing consistently in our own documentation projects on languages from the Permic and Saamic branches: (1) Use an orthography-based transcription system; this not only allows quicker and more efficient transcription of field recordings, but it makes it possible to easily integrate all available (digitized) printed texts into the corpus. In addition, any available (digitized) lexical resources can be integrated into the annotation tools under creation as well, rather than building new dictionaries from scratch via interlinearization. (2) Apply computer-based methods as much as possible in creating higher-level annotations of the compiled corpus data.

The examples in our paper are taken specifically from Komi-Zyrian, an endangered Uralic language. Other endangered Uralic languages we work on at present are Akkala Saami, Kildin Saami, Pite Saami, Skolt Saami and Ter Saami. We present our work-in-progress concerning the application of rule-based morphological tagging and syntactic disambiguation in order to automatically create higher-level corpus annotations. In this, our aim is to challenge and further develop current approaches at the interface between computational, descriptive and documentary linguistics of endangered languages.

---

[10]For printed sources from the Soviet Union and earlier, the Fenno-Ugrica Collection is especially relevant: `http://fennougrica.kansalliskirjasto.fi`; contemporary printed sources are also systematically digitized, e.g. for both Komi languages: `http://komikyv.ru/`.

[11]See, for instance, The Finno-Ugric Languages and The Internet Project [14].

2　Spoken corpus annotation

The dominating paradigm within computational linguistics is based on statistical methods and training a computer to understand the behavior of natural language by means of presenting it with vast amounts of either unanalyzed or manually analyzed data. However, for the majority of the world's languages, and especially for low-resourced endangered languages, this approach is not a viable option because the amounts of texts that would be required – analyzed or not – are typically not available. The competing paradigm is a rule-based ("grammar-based") analysis: a linguist writes a machine-readable version of the grammar, and compiles it into a program capable of analyzing (and eventually also generating) text input. There are several schools within the rule-based paradigm; the approach chosen by our projects uses a combination of finite-state transducer technology for morphological analyses, and Constraint Grammar for the syntactic analyses.

This approach has been tested for several written languages, and it routinely provides highly robust analyses for unconstrained text input. We adapt the open-source preprocessing and analysis toolkit provided by the Giellatekno project [16][12] for both written and spoken, transcribed language data. Since the Giellatekno infrastructure is built for standard written languages, we have developed a set of conventions for converting our spoken language data into a "written-like" format that is thus more easily portable into the Giellatekno infrastructure. First, we represent our spoken recordings in standardized orthography (with adaptations for dialectal and other sub-standard forms when needed), rather than in phonemic transcription (this is unlike many other endangered language documentation projects). Second, we mark clause boundaries and use other punctuation marks as in written language, even though surface text structuring in spoken texts is prosodic rather than syntactic and the alignment of our texts to the original recording is utterance-based, rather than sentence-based. For specific spoken-language phenomena, such as false starts, hesitations or self-corrections as well as when marking incomprehensible sections in our transcription, we use a simple (and orthography-compatible) markup adapted from annotation conventions commonly used in spoken language corpora.[13] Different resources on endangered languages have typically used different transcription conventions and orthographies, and essentially our approach using orthography is based on the idea that we should select a single system for transcriptions. The current orthography is the most established one of the different variants, and is used for the the largest amount of available texts. The orthographies on the languages we work with are relatively phonemic, al-

---

[12]Giellatekno, The Center for Saami Language Technology (University of Tromsø), `http://giellatekno.uit.no/`

[13]Our convention is based on HIAT [17], but is much simpler and only includes a few rules.

though the Cyrillic writing system and borrowed Russian conventions lead to a few additional cosmetic details. However, it still represents the underlying phoneme level very well, and any texts using more narrow transcriptions can always be converted to the orthography; at the same time, virtually all other transcription systems used can be transliterated into the orthographic representation as they generally still adhere to the same phoneme level. In addition, using orthography makes our transcriptions readily accessible to the language community because speakers are used to reading in orthography; this even makes it easier to employ native speakers to work on transcribing the segmented audio data.

The annotation process works on three levels:

(1) The first level is a preprocessor which tokenizes the orthographic transcription.

(2) The second level is a morphological analyzer, programmed as a finite-state transducer (FST) for modeling free and bound morphemes as well as linear and non-linear rules according to which morphemes combine in word formation and inflection: the upper side of the resulting transducer consists of a lemma and a string of grammatical tags for each word form, while the lower side contains the concatenation of stem, affixes, and markers signaling suprasegmental rules. The lower side of the transducer is fed to a so-called Two-Level-Morphology (TWOL) component [18] used for handling complex suprasegmental morphophonological rules (which are particularly characteristic of the Saamic languages, but much less so of Komi).

(3) The third level is a syntactic analyzer-disambiguator, written as a set of rules following Constraint Grammar (CG). The lack of a higher-level analysis often leads to cases of ambiguity concerning the morphological analysis, i.e., multiple analyses for one and the same word form, which is of course problematic since any given token has a single correct morphological analysis. For the syntactic disambiguation of these homonyms, we use CG, which takes the morphologically analyzed text as its input, and ideally only returns the appropriate reading. CG is a language-independent formalism for morphological disambiguation and syntactic analysis of text corpora developed by [19, 20]. The CG analysis can be enriched with syntactic functions and dependency relations if all underlying grammatical rules are described sufficiently. Since the output of a CG analysis is a dependency structure for a particular sentence, the output may also be converted into phrase structure representations, cf. the example in Figure 1. Similar to other projects using the Giellatekno toolkit, we use VISLCG-3 for the compilation of the manually written CG rules [21].[14]

The following examples illustrate a possible case of homonymy to be disambiguated after the FST morphological analysis.

    1. сёй : сёй+N+Sg+Nom

---

[14]VISLCG-3 is an improved version of VISL, documented at http://beta.visl.sdu.dk/cg3.html.

2. сёй : сёйны+V+ConNeg

3. сёй : сёйны+V+Imprt+Sg2

Here, the token to be analyzed is сёй. The analyzer spells out the possible lemmas сёй 'clay' and сёйны 'to eat' followed by the possible part-of-speech and morphological category tags for a total of three theoretically possible readings. One example of a (relatively simple) syntactic rule used in the disambiguation of a token сёй would be:

- IFF: ConNeg if Neg to the left

This rule would apply when the token сёй follows a negation verb inside running text, thus selecting the second analysis as the correct one in such a case.

Our work with the CG description of Komi is still at an initial stage. For the Saamic languages, we have not started work with CG yet. To be completed, it would likely need to include several thousand rules. However, the experience of other Giellate-kno projects working with CG shows that some months of concentrated work can result in a CG description that can already be implemented in a preliminary tagger useful for lexicographic work as well as for several other purposes. For instance, the rather shallow grammar parser for Southern Saami described by [22] includes only somewhat more than 100 CG rules, but already results in reasonably good lemmatization accuracy for open-class parts-of-speech. This means that the approach is readily adaptable for language documentation projects with limited resources. Furthermore, CG rules can potentially be ported from one language to another, e.g. the rule described above for disambiguating the connegative verb in Komi would also work for several other Uralic languages.

3   Summary

Although endangered language documentation has a focus on multi-modal speech corpora and uses data from small orally transmitted languages, the relevant research is in essence similar to corpus building of any other non-endangered and/or written language. However, endangered language documentation does not seem to be well informed by common theories known from "non-endangered corpus linguistics" and typically does not even consider using computational methods for corpus annotation and the creation of qualitatively and quantitatively more significant corpora. Why do the majority of endangered language documentation projects still rely entirely on non-automated methods if NLP has already been applied successfully to very small languages?[15] A possible answer is that many linguists working with language documentation come from comparative and descriptive linguistics and prefer qualitative methods. The approach described in our paper tries to consistently apply proven methods from NLP in endangered language documentation and potentially even in endangered language description.

While rule-based morphosyntactic modeling is initially time-consuming (at the development stage), it does have significant advantages: (1) the results of automatic tagging are exceptionally precise and consistent, and – obviously – automatic; (2) while incrementally formulating rules and testing them on the corpus data, we are not only creating a tool but producing a full-fledged grammatical description based on broad empirical evidence at the same time; and last but not least (3) our work can eventually even help develop new language technology for computer-aided teaching and writing. For instance, our FST descriptions are implemented in the creation of spell-checkers using the Giellatekno toolkit.

Due to the fact that significant official support and language planning activities currently exist for Komi as well as some of the other languages we are working on, these languages are increasingly used in spoken and written form. Better adaptation of computational technology by researchers working in the field of language documentation will in the long run become necessary in order to more efficiently annotate and make effective use of the increasing amount of data available.

Whereas the rule-based methods described in this paper have already been successfully used with *written* varieties of Komi and Saamic languages, our paper describes their application specifically to *spoken* varieties. This approach is a novelty in the field of language documentation and computational linguistics for small Uralic languages and not at all a trivial task. It requires innovative research for several reasons: (1) specific spoken-language phenomena (false starts, self-corrections, incomprehensible speech, etc.) marked in transcriptions need to be pre-processed systematically; (2) additional morphological and syntactic rules need to be introduced to process linguistic variation characteristic of spoken varieties; and last but not least (3) our corpus data is often not monolingual, but instead includes a significant amount of borrowings from Russian or other relevant majority languages for other projects as well as code-switching into these languages.

This last point is worth explaining in more detail because it addresses a potential (and obviously necessary) direction to take in the future of automatic corpus annotation of spoken Uralic language data. As mentioned above, we use orthographic transcriptions consistently, even for non-target languages present in our corpus data,

---

[15]This question was asked by Arienne Dwyer in a recent project description, `http://www.nsf.gov/awardsearch/showAward?AWD_ID=1519164`.

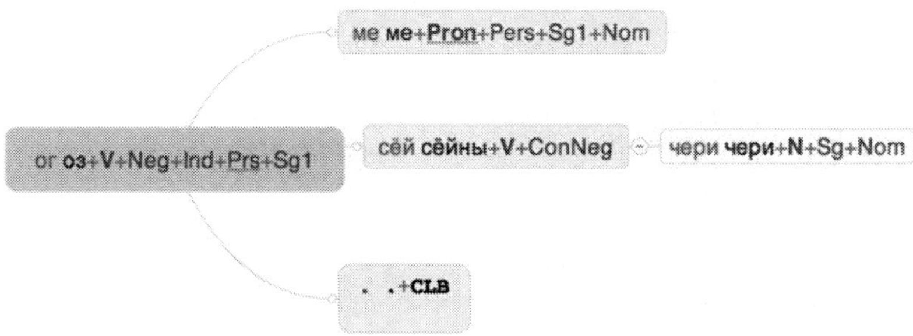

Figure 1: Dependency tree for the Komi sentence *Ме чери ог сёй.* "I don't eat fish" after disambiguation

i.e., switches to Russian and Tundra Nenets. Since analyzers for Russian and Tundra Nenets are also available in the Giellatekno infrastructure, we can run multiple language analysis easily. This is a direct benefit and consequence of adopting the pre-existing Giellatekno infrastructure and of using orthographies in transcription. As a result, it becomes possible to automatically detect the parts of our corpus where multiple languages occur. Because of the rule-based approach requires all combinations of free and bound morphemes to be detected in the corresponding lexica and rules, this works best when switches between languages are indisputable (rather than ad hoc borrowings or other hybrid forms). While the handling of mixed language data in our corpora is not yet entirely worked out, we can already use this approach for concrete tasks, such as for assigning language tags to different recordings. Improved methods for automatically detecting code-mixing and code-switching and then merging the resulting analyses, are in the works.

References

[1] Nikolaus Himmelmann. Language documentation. What is it and what is it good for? In Jost Gippert, Ulrike Mosel, and Nikolaus Himmelmann, editors, *Essentials of Language Documentation*, number 178 in Trends in Linguistics. Studies and Monographs, pages 1–30. Mouton de Gruyter, Berlin, 2006.

[2] Anthony C. Woodbury. Language documentation. In Peter K. Austin and Julia Sallabank, editors, *The Cambridge handbook of endangered languages*, Cam-

bridge handbooks in language and linguistics, pages 159–186. Cambridge University Press, Cambridge, 2011.

[3] Nikolaus P. Himmelmann. Linguistic data types and the interface between language documentation and description. *Language Documentation & Conservation*, 6:187–207, 2012. URL: http://hdl.handle.net/10125/4503.

[4] Peter K. Austin. Language documentation in the 21st century. *JournaLIPP*, 3:57–71, 2014. URL: http://lipp.ub.lmu.de/article/download/190/83.

[5] Trond Trosterud. Grammar-based language technology for the Sámi languages. In *Lesser used Languages & Computer Linguistics*, pages 133–148. Europäische Akademie, Bozen, 2006.

[6] Thierry Poibeau and Benjamin Fagard. Exploring natural language processing methods for Finno-Ugric languages. In Tommi A. Pirinen, Francis M. Tyers, and Trond Trosterud, editors, *Second International Workshop on Computational Linguistics for Uralic Languages, 20th January, 2016, Szeged, Hungary. Proceedings of the workshop*. Volume 2016. University of Szeged, 2016. In press.

[7] *SIKOR. UiT The Arctic University of Norway and the Norwegian Saami Parliament's Saami text collection, Version 08.12.2016.* Tromsø, 2016. URL: http://gtweb.uit.no/korp.

[8] Rogier Blokland, Ciprian Gerstenberger, Marina Fedina, Niko Partanen, Michael Rießler, and Joshua Wilbur. Language documentation meets language technology. In Tommi A. Pirinen, Francis M. Tyers, and Trond Trosterud, editors, *First International Workshop on Computational Linguistics for Uralic Languages, 16th January, 2015, Tromsø, Norway. Proceedings of the workshop*. Volume 2015, number 2 in Septentrio Conference Series, pages 8–18. The University Library of Tromsø, Tromsø, 2015. DOI: 10.7557/scs.2015.2.

[9] Wagner-Nagy Beáta and Sándor Szeverényi. Linguistically annotated spoken Nganasan corpus. *Tomsk Journal of Linguistics and Anthropology*, 2:25–33, 2015.

[10] Bernard Comrie, Andrey Shluinsky, and Olesya Khanina. Documentation of Enets. Digitization and analysis of legacy field materials and fieldwork with last speakers. In *The Endangered Language Archive (ELAR)*. SOAS University of London, London, 2005-2017. URL: https://elar.soas.ac.uk/Collection/MPI950079.

[11]   Andrey Filchenko and Balthasar Bickel. Comprehensive documentation and analysis of two endangered Siberian languages. Eastern Khanty and Southern Selkup. In *The Endangered Language Archive (ELAR)*. SOAS University of London, London, [n.d.]–2017. URL: https://elar.soas.ac.uk/Collection/MPI43298.

[12]   Eszter Simon and Nikolett Mus. Languages under the influence. Building a database of Uralic languages. In Tommi A. Pirinen, Francis M. Tyers, and Trond Trosterud, editors, *Third International Workshop on Computational Linguistics for Uralic languages, 23rd January, Saint Petersburg/Russia. Proceedings of the workshop*. 2017. In press.

[13]   Beata Wagner-Nagy, Hanna Hedeland, Timm Lehmberg, and Michael Rießler. INEL. Eine Infrastruktur zur Dokumentation indigener nordeurasischer Sprachen. In *Konferenz "Forschungsdaten in den Geisteswissenschaften (FORGE 2015)". 15. bis 18. September 2015 an der Universität Hamburg*. Lecture2Go. Projekt Geisteswissenschaftliche Infrastruktur für Nachhaltigkeit (gwin), Hamburg, 2015. URL: https://lecture2go.uni-hamburg.de/l2go/-/get/v/18306.

[14]   Heidi Jauhiainen, Tommi Jauhiainen, and Krister Lindén. The Finno-Ugric Languages and The Internet Project. In Tommi A. Pirinen, Francis M. Tyers, and Trond Trosterud, editors, *First International Workshop on Computational Linguistics for Uralic Languages, 16th January, 2015, Tromsø, Norway. Proceedings of the workshop*. Volume 2015, number 2 in Septentrio Conference Series, pages 87–98. The University Library of Tromsø, Tromsø, 2015. DOI: 10.7557/5.3471.

[15]   Timofey Arkhangelskiy and Maria Medvedeva. Developing morphologically annotated corpora for minority languages of russia. In Sandra Kübler and Markus Dickinson, editors, *Proceedings of Corpus Linguistics Fest 2016. Bloomington, IN, USA, June 6-10, 2016*. Pages 1–6, 2016.

[16]   Sjur Moshagen, Tommi A. Pirinen, and Trond Trosterud. Building an open-source development infrastructure for language technology projects. In *Proceedings of the 19th Nordic Conference of Computational Linguistics NODALIDA*, number 16 in NEALT Proceedings Series, pages 343–352, 2013.

[17]   Jochen Rehbein, Thomas Schmidt, Bernd Meyer, Franziska Watzke, and Annette Herkenrath. *Handbuch für das computergestützte Transkribieren nach HIAT*, number 56 in Arbeiten zur Mehrsprachigkeit, Folge B. Universität Hamburg, Hamburg, 2004. URL: http://www.exmaralda.org/files/azm_56.pdf.

[18] Sjur Moshagen, Trond Trosterud, and Pekka Sammallahti. Twol at work. In Antti Arppe, Lauri Carlson, Krister Lindén, Jussi Piitulainen, Mickael Suominen, Martti Vainio, Hanna Westerlund, and Anssi Yli-Jyrä, editors, *Inquiries into Words, Constraints and Contexts*, pages 94–105. CSLI, Stanford, 2008.

[19] Fred Karlsson. Constraint Grammar as a framework for parsing unrestricted text. In Hans Karlgren, editor, *Proceedings of the 13th International Conference of Computational Linguistics*. Volume 3, pages 168–173. Helsinki, 1990.

[20] Fred Karlsson, Atro Voutilainen, Juha Heikkilä, and Arto Anttila, editors. *Constraint Grammar. A language-independent system for parsing unrestricted text*, number 4 in Natural Language Processing. Mouton de Gruyter, Berlin, 1995.

[21] Tino Didriksen. *Constraint grammar manual. 3rd version of the CG formalism variant*. GrammarSoft ApS, 2007–2016. URL: http://visl.sdu.dk/cg3/vislcg3.pdf.

[22] Lene Antonsen and Trond Trosterud. Next to nothing – a cheap South Saami disambiguator. In Eckhard Bick, Kristin Hagen, Kaili Müürisep, and Trond Trosterud, editors, *Proceedings of the NODALIDA 2011 Workshop Constraint Grammar Applications, May 11, 2011 Riga, Latvia*, number 14 in NEALT Proceedings Series, pages 1–7. Tartu University Library, Tartu, 2011. URL: http://hdl.handle.net/10062/19296.

[23] Tommi A. Pirinen, Francis M. Tyers, and Trond Trosterud, editors. First International Workshop on Computational Linguistics for Uralic Languages, 16th January, 2015, Tromsø, Norway. Volume 2015. (2) in Septentrio Conference Series. The University Library of Tromsø, Tromsø, 2015.

Preliminary Experiments in the Extraction of Predicative Structures from a Large Finnish Corpus

Guersande Chaminade
CNRS & ENS & PSL & Université Sorbonne nouvelle & USPC
LATTICE Lab. & INaLCO
1 rue Maurice Arnoux 92120 Montrouge France
`gu.chaminade@gmail.com`

Thierry Poibeau
CNRS & ENS & PSL & Université Sorbonne nouvelle & USPC
LATTICE Lab.
1 rue Maurice Arnoux 92120 Montrouge France
`thierry.poibeau@ens.fr`

Abstract

This paper presents different experiments aiming at automatically extracting lexical information from corpora. We first describe a simple experiment on the nature of direct objects in Finnish (partitive vs total objects) so as to check if data automatically extracted from corpora support traditional studies in the field. Which are the verbs subcategorizing partitive objects? Which are the verbs subcategorizing (more frequently) total objects? We provide a tool and a user interface to browse data automatically collected from a large corpus in order to make it possible to answer this question. We then describe some ongoing work aiming at adapting to Finnish a complex lexical acquisition system initially developed for Japanese [1]. In our approach, following up on studies in natural language processing and linguistics, we embrace the double hypothesis: *i)* of a continuum between ambiguity and vagueness, and *ii)* of a continuum between arguments and adjuncts. We describe the system developed for the task and conclude with some perspectives for the evaluation of the produced resource.

The 3rd International Workshop for Computational Linguistics of Uralic Languages, pages 37–55,
St. Petersburg, Russia, 23–24 January 2017. ©2017 Association for Computational Linguistics

1   Introduction

Natural language processing traditionally requires precise and high coverage resources to provide satisfactory results but it is well known that the development of such resources is long and costly. Recently machine learning has made it possible to develop resources at a lower cost. It is now possible to automatically analyse large corpora, typically made of several million words, and develop parsers based on the observation of surface regularities at corpus level, along with some annotated data used for training. Powerful unlexicalized parsers have been developed for several languages, with a surprisingly high accuracy given the fact no lexical information is provided in input [2, 3].

The output of these parsers has subsequently been used as a new source of knowledge for the development of large-scale lexical resources. This area of research, known as lexical acquisition, have permitted the development of large-scale dictionaries for example for English [4], French [5], Japanese [1] and lots of other languages as well. It has also been shown that the approach provides interesting (although not perfect) results: thanks to this approach, it for example possible to discover new subcategorization frames for particular verbs [6, 7] and to monitor in real time the evolution of word usage or the creation of new words in a language [1], etc. Results obtained with automatic methods are of course still far from perfect: they need to be manually checked but they usually provide lots of new results and new sources of evidence for further work. One of the most obvious application is probably the fact that automatic methods make it possible to complete existing resources at a lower cost, so as to obtain a better coverage [6]. Automatic methods also provide statistical information, which is a key element for any computational linguistic system nowadays.

We think these approaches are important for linguistic analysis as well. Too often, natural language processing only focuses on practical applications, which are of course very important for the field. But we think it can also be highly valuable to use automatic tools to provide results based on large-scale analysis to linguists, who could then base their analyses on data that is otherwise hard to process directly.

Therefore, we describe in this paper different experiments concerning verb subcategorization frames in Finnish. Our goal is twofold:

1. provide tools and data for linguists, based on the analysis of large corpora. Linguists are for example interested in the study of differential object marking in Finnish: which verbs subcategorize partitive complements? Which verbs subcategorize total (accusative) objects? Which verbs subcategorize both kinds of complements? Although lots of studies have already explored this question, technology provides today an easy way to obtain quantified data computed over

very large corpora and thus may shed new light on such topics as differential object marking in Finnish (or any other Finno-Ugric language since the method can easily be transferred to another language).

2. use advanced clustering techniques to observe large-scale verb families based on their usage in corpora. Based on the hypothesis put forward by Levin [8], we think that, to a certain extent at least, syntactic behaviour can serve as a footstep to semantics. More precisely, we want to cluster verbs having the same syntactic behaviour and observe if in doing so we get relatively homogeneous semantic classes as a result.

The resource comes along with a user interface making it possible to navigate the data: we think a lexical resource should not be frozen but should be easily adaptable depending on the user need. More specifically we want the end user to be able to navigate and explore the data so as to get more or less fine-grained lexical descriptions in the lexicon.

The paper is structured as follows. We first give a quick overview of previous work in lexical acquisition. We then provide a brief reminder of Finnish objects and grammatical cases in Finnish. The following section describes the analysis of our corpus (the Finnish section of the Europarl corpus) using the Turku Parser [9] and how relevant information is identified and extracted. The following section describes the Web interface giving access to corpus information about the nature of objects (total vs partitive) depending on the verb considered. The last section describes some ongoing work on the extraction of families of verb constructions using clustering techniques. We describe how the system is derived from a previous implementation for Japanese [1], with of course an adaptation of all the language-dependent modules to Finnish.

2 Previous Work

The first works in automatic lexical acquisition date back to the early 1990s. The need for precise and comprehensive lexical databases was clearly identified as a major need for most NLP tasks (esp. parsing) and automatic acquisition techniques was then seen as a way to solve the resource bottleneck. However, the first experiments [10, 11] were limited (the acquisition process was dealing with a few verbs only and a limited number of predefined subcategorization frames). They were based on local heuristics and did not take into account the wider context.

The approach was then refined so as to take into account all the most frequent verbs and subcategorization frames possible [12, 13, 14]. A last innovation consisted in letting the system infer the subcategorization frames directly from the corpus, without having to predefined the list of possible frames. This approach is supposed to be less precise than the previous one, but most errors can be automatically filtered out since they tend to produce patterns with a very low frequency. Most experiments so far have been made on verbs (since verbs are supposed to have the most complex subcategorization frames), but the approach can also be extended to nouns and adjectives without too many problems [4].

Most developments so far have been done on English, but more and more experiments are now done for other languages as well (see for example, experiments on French [5], German [15], Chinese [16], or Japanese [1] among many others). The quality of the result depends of course on the kind of corpus used for acquisition, and even more on the considered language and on the size of the corpus used. Dictionaries obtained with very large corpora form the Web generally give the best performances. The availability of accurate unlexicalized parser is also a key feature for the quality of the acquisition process.

To the best of our knowledge, there has not been any large-scale experiment for Finnish yet. However we are lucky to have access to large corpora of Finnish, as well as to relevant parsers. For our experiments on Finnish, we have used the Finnish part of the Finnish-English pair of the Europarl corpus ($6th$ version of the parallel corpus, `http://www.statmt.org/europarl/`), containing more than 29 million words. Europarl is a corpus extracted from the proceedings of the European Parliament between 1997 and 2011. The corpus addresses heterogeneous topics, which makes it possible to acquire a quite varied lexicon, although the style of the corpus is quite regular and formal.

In the near future we plan to use bigger corpora that are now available, especially the Turku Dependency Treebank (TDT) [9] that consists of 181K tokens and 13.5K sentences. Bigger corpora allow one to cover different verb usage and more verbs, since it is necessary to get a minimum number of occurrences in order to provide relevant information. The contrast between partitive and total objects can already be observed taking a threshold of 10 or 15 occurrences of a given verb (but more occurrences will of course give more robust and accurate results). For verb clustering, it seems hard to get relevant results for less than 100 occurrences per verb.

3   Finnish object and grammatical cases

We base our description on the general and widely available Finnish grammar by Fred Karlsson [17].

Finnish is (among many other things) characterized by a linguistic phenomenon called "differential object marking". In other words, the object of a given verb may be marked by different cases, depending on the verb, the noun and the overall meaning one wants to convey. The basic opposition is between partitive objects and accusative (or "total") objects.

Partitive object occurs in three instances:

1. in negative sentences,
2. when the action expressed by the verb is irresultative,
3. when the object expresses an indefinite quantity. [17]

We have to take into account quantifiers since with a quantifier, the case does not depend on the verb but on the quantifier. We also chose to isolate negative verbal structures, since partitive is then mandatory for the object, thus neutralizing the free opposition between partitive and total object.

Along with partitive objects, Finnish also has another kind of direct complement known as accusative (or "total object"). The accusative expresses:

1. a resultative action,
2. a whole or a definite quantity in affirmative sentences.

According to [17], in Finnish "the accusative is not a uniform morphological case form as such, but a collective name given to a certain set of cases when they mark the object of the sentence. These cases are: nominative singular, which of course has no ending (Ø); genitive singular, with the ending -n; the -t accusative ending peculiar to personal pronouns; and the nominative plural in -t. The accusative, i.e. this set of case forms, appears as the case of the object in opposition to the partitive".

The object takes t-accusative in the following cases : the object is a pronoun, the object is total (in which case, it takes accusative plural, identical to the nominative plural). The object takes n-accusative in all other cases. The object takes nominative when the object is a total object in a passive construction (identical to non-marked accusative), or an object of a verb conjugated in the imperative.

Karlsson [17] formalizes this through the three following rules:

1. The -t accusative always marks the object
   (a) in the plural
   (b) in personal pronouns.

2. A singular accusative object
   (a) usually takes -n
   (b) takes no ending with verbs in first and second person imperative, passive verbs, and some verbs of obligation

3. Numerals (except yksi 'one') have no accusative ending.

Karlsson [17] also says that "when determining the particular case of the object one must first check whether any of the conditions for the partitive hold; if so, the object must be in the partitive. The partitive is thus a 'stronger' object case than the accusative. Only after this, if none of the partitive object conditions are fulfilled, can one proceed to determine which of the accusative endings is the correct one".

The case of the object is therefore accusative only if (a) the sentence is affirmative, and also (b) the action of the verb is resultative, or (c) the object is a whole or a definite quantity. With respect to (c), the accusative may be compared to the nominative when the nominative marks the subject

4 Verbal structure extraction

In this section, we describe how the corpus is analysed with the Turku Parser and how relevant information is automatically extracted for further analysis.

4.1 The parser

The first step consists in analysing the corpus so as to be able to identify the main relations between words. We chose to use the Turku parser as described in [18]. This is probably he most accurate parser for Finnish currently available.

For each sentence, the parser produces a tree where the main verb is the root. According to Haverinen et al. [9] "the annotation scheme of the treebank is a Finnish-specific version of the well-known Stanford Dependency (SD) scheme, originally developed by de Marneffe and Manning [19, 20]. The SD scheme represents the syntax of a sentence as a graph where the nodes represent the words of the sentence, and the edges represent directed dependencies between them. One of the two words connected by a dependency is the head or governor while the other is the dependent. Each dependency is labelled with a dependency type, which describes the syntactic function of the dependent word".

Results reported in the [9] are "97.3% POS and 94.8% PM" (correct part-of-speech tags / correct part of speech tags + morphological information) and [18] gives results around .86 UAS and LAS (nodes that have the correct incoming arc / node that have the correct incoming arc with the correct label, i.e. the right syntactic tag).

The output has to be slightly modified so as to fit with our problem. The following mappings are defined : N-accusative matches genitive, T-Accusative matches accusative, non-marked accusative matches nominative (and partitive is partitive). Hence in this context, a partitive object takes the partitive case, and a total object

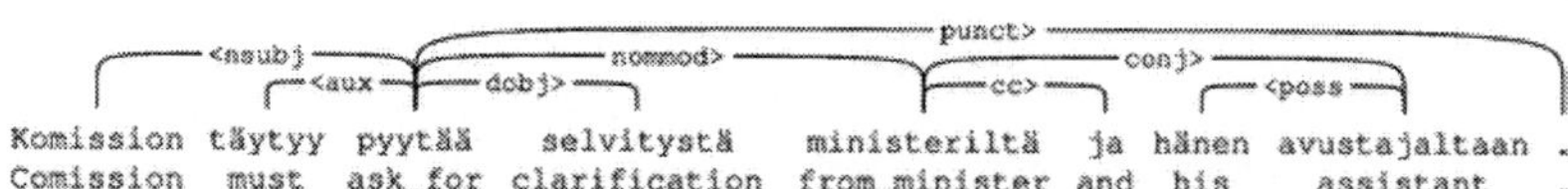

Figure 1: An example taken from [9] using the Stanford dependency scheme. The sentence can be translated as *"The commission must ask for clarification from the minister and his assistant."*

takes either the genitive, or the accusative (or the nominative, although we mostly limited the process to the active voice).

4.2 Verb structure extraction from the CONLL format

The goal here is to generate a list of predicative structures, each containing three elements: the verb, its complements and the case used for each complement. The program takes as input a CONLL format file, which is the output by the Turku parser. The CONLL format is very convenient for this kind of extraction, as shown in the example below (the two empty slots were originally used to contain gold-standard data) :

```
1 kauden     kausi      NOUN _ Case=Gen|Nb=Sing 2 nmod:poss _ 1.1
2 avaaminen avaaminen NOUN _ Case=Nom|Nb=Sing 0 root      _ 1.1
3 on ...
```

Each line corresponds to one word (aka one lexical entry), and contains the following list of information :

1. an index referring to the word,
2. the inflected form (i. e. the form as it appears in the original text),
3. the corresponding lemma,
4. the POS tag (Universal Dependencies),
5. (empty)
6. morphological features,
7. the index of the word's governor / head (for root elements, this value is 0),
8. the dependency relation ,
9. (empty)
10. an index referring to the sentence where the word appears.

Since each line is a tabulation-separated list, it is quite simple to split it into an easy to handle data structure on which grammatical filters are applied. The CONLL09 format is also handy when it comes to transcribe the filters into sets of selection constraints. To give a very simple example, we state that for a word to be a verb (and thus be selected), the fourth item in the list must be the string 'VERB' (other restrictions are applied, as discussed in what follows).

4.3 Retrieving predicative structures from the CONLL09 format

We extract verbal structures that correspond to different selection criteria expressed though constraints. Verbal structure extraction happens only if both the expectations on the verb and on the complement are met. To achieve this, we use the following selection of constraints on the verb:

- the POS tag is 'VERB',

- the clause must be an independent clause or a subordinate clause (i.e. not an infinitive or participle clause),

- as for mood restriction, it is possible to choose between indicative, conditional and imperative; negative forms of the verb can also be selected but these forms are processed separately;

- finally, the voice of the verb can be active or passive.

These characteristics are then 'transcribed' in the CONLL09 format:

- the POS tag is the fourth slot of the data structure concerning the verb, so this constraint becomes data[3]='VERB'.

- since the verb is the root element of its clause, the nature of the clause is described using the dependency relationship of the verb. Thus the different possibilities are given as a list. Technically, things look like: extract data in ('root', 'ccomp', 'xcomp'), where 'root' corresponds to an independent clause, 'ccomp' to a subordinate clause, and 'xcomp' to a subordinate clause without its own subject.

- depending on which constraints one wants to use, the query is:

  - for the indicative and conditional modes: 'Mood=Ind','Mood=Cnd',

- for the imperative mood: 'Mood=Imp',

- if one only wants to work on negative / non-negative forms, a 'Connegative=Yes' feature is available,

- the voice of the verb can be either active 'Voice=Act', or passive 'Voice= Pass'.

5 Observing differential object marking in Finnish based on corpus data

In this experiment we are only interested in objects depending directly on the verb: the goal here is to classify verbs depending on the case they use for their direct object. Negative sentences (i.e. sentences with a negation) are excluded since the negation automatically entails the use of the partitive for the object.

5.1 Description of the Approach

The classification of verbs is done according to three categories:

1. verbs subcategorizing exclusively the partitive case,

2. verbs subcategorizing exclusively the accusative / genitive case,

3. verbs subcategorizing both cases.

The idea is to find under (1) and (2) verbs that impose specific constraints to their object, thus neutralizing the possible opposition between partitive and total objects, while verbs in the third category (3) are supposed to be really subject to differential object marking. Practically, we categorize a verb as a partitive object verb, if at least 85% of the direct objects appearing with this verb are marked with the partitive. We categorize a verb as a 'total object' verb, if at least 65% of the objects are marked with the genitive / accusative. Other verbs are categorized as mixed object verbs. These thresholds have been fixed empirically and can be modified. The threshold is not the same for the different categories because more verbs have partitive objects due to semantic reasons that are not directly connected to aspectual oppositions (for example when the object denotes an imprecise quantity that constrains the use of the partitive).

The case of (1) and (2) should be monitored thoroughly since (1) for example also contains verbs for which £total objects' can be found but in small quantities.

Technically, the verb complement must be either direct or indirect object ('dobj', 'iobj'). All the results are stored in a file that is accessible through a simple Web interface.

The following results are obtained using the Europarl corpus described above: 439 total object verbs, 1 269 partitive object verbs, and 683 mixed object verbs. These results are obtained without taking into account verb frequency. In order to obtain more reliable results we did some experiments with different thresholds.

- With a threshold of 20 instances, we get 61 total object verbs, 316 partitive object verbs, and 209 mixed object verbs.

- With a threshold of 50 instances, we get 49 total object verbs, 205 partitive object verbs, and 142 mixed object verbs.

- With a threshold of 100 instances, we get 34 total object verbs, 148 partitive object verbs, and 95 mixed object verbs.

These results show the great number of verbs appearing only a few times in the corpus: from 2436 without threshold, the total number of verbs falls to only 586 with a threshold of 20, 396 with a threshold of 50, and 277 with a threshold of 100. This is a direct consequence of the type of text used in this experiment: there are many different topics discussed during the European Parliament sessions, and only relatively frequent verbs remain when we increase the frequency threshold.

Table 1: Number of verbs depending on the frequency threshold.

Threshold	Verbs	Total Object		Partitive Object		Mixed	
20	586	61	10.4%	316	53.9%	209	35.7%
50	396	49	12,4%	205	51.7%	142	35,9%
100	277	34	12.3%	148	53.4%	95	34,3%

However, note that the results are rather stable once the less frequent verbs are removed. Partitive object verbs always represent more than half of the total, and thus outnumber the two other categories; mixed objects verbs always outnumber total object verbs (these two observations are also true if no threshold is set, as one can see from the figures given previously).

5.2   Results and Evaluation

The result of the classification is presented in a Web interface that shows the three categories (verbs mainly subcategorizing total objects, verbs mainly subcategorizing partitive objects, and verbs subcategorizing both kinds of objects).

The different categories are represented as columns, each one with a different colour: orange for total object verbs, blue for partitive object verbs and green for mixed object verbs. Moreover each verb entry is associated with different information: the list of the most frequent nouns subcategorized by the verb, a few typical examples, etc. It is also possible to look for a specific verb in the database. Figure 2 shows an overview of the graphical interface with some examples displayed for *ymmärtää*.

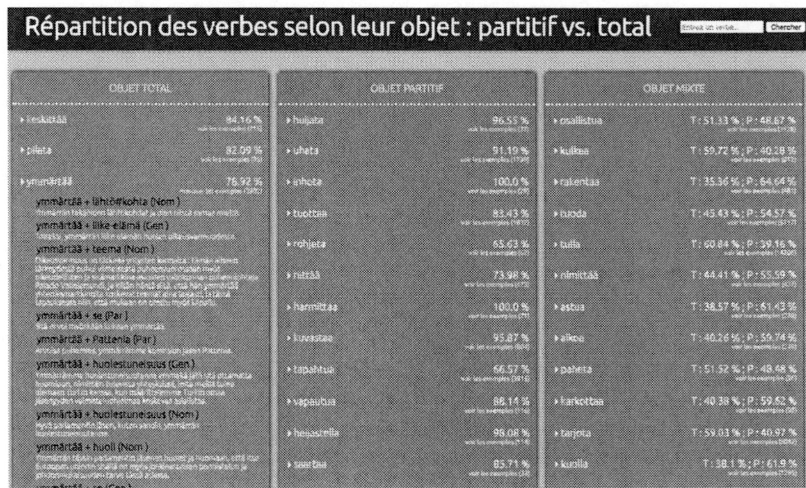

Figure 2: Web interface showing the different verbs sorted in three categories

The interface also provides information on other possible subcategorization frames for each verb. This is not the primary goal of this interface but it makes it possible for lexicographers to have a quick overview of the diversity of possible constructions for each verb.

Our first experiments with end-users prove that this tool is useful for linguists and lexicographers to check the behaviour of verbs in different contexts. It is also useful for professors and even more students learning Finnish, since the interface provides a large number of examples. Most of the time the verb frames observed in the Europarl corpus support the traditional descriptions found in dictionarires (e.g. "*harmittaa*" subcategorizes the partitive, "*Minua harmittaa kuitenkin se, että...*", "*Tämä harmittaa minua.*", etc.) but language learners may be surprised by certain facts, like the proportion of total objects (i.e. nominative / genitive / accusative objects) for a verb like *ymmärtää*. For several language learners, *ymmärtää* is irresultative and should thus require the use of the partitive case, which is far from being true (e.g. "*Ymmärrämme tämän välttämättömän keskustelun taustat.*", "*Kansalainen ymmärtää nyt EU:n.*").

Our system just extracts information from the output of the Turku parser and thus should not make errors in itself. We noted a few errors in the output of the Turku NLP system2. When these errors were a problem for our analysis, we added some constraints to the extraction algorithm (for example, we noted a frequent error with lexical forms ending with '*-mme*', especially between the verbal and the possessive suffix. This was filtered out by the extraction algorithm).

6   Towards large-scale lexical acquisition for Finnish

Our goal is now to extend the work to the whole argument structure of the verb, following the line of research described in the state-of-the-art section. The input is the same very large corpus of raw text that is parsed by the unlexicalized Turku parser for Finnish (it is necessary to use an unlexicalized parser since we want to learn subcategorization frames and we do not want the process to be biased by pre-defined resources). By observing regularities at surface level, it is possible to infer subcategorization frames, i.e. infer the most probable constructions, separate arguments and adjuncts (also called modifiers) and have statistical information about the possible complements of a given verb.

We re-use the pipeline developed initially by Pierre Marchal for Japanese [21, 1, 22]. Since the original linguistic pipeline was built to study predicative structures extracted from Japanese, all language-dependent modules had to be changed and adapted to Finnish. This was mostly true for the initial linguistic pipeline: we used the Turku parser for this, as explained above. All the clustering modules (that are language-independent) have been used as they were in the original implementation.

As for grammatical cases, we considered the following cases: partitive, genitive, accusative (traditional object cases), locative cases (inessive, elative, illative, adessive, ablative and allative), and translative (we do not necessarily exclude other cases, although they appear less frequently except the nominative in passive structures).

We slightly modified the original interface to add examples that illustrate the different produced clusters. We think this is necessary because the end user can vary, via two sliders, two thresholds corresponding to two parameters. The first corresponds to the minimum distance between the minimal classes obtained with the first classification step. The second corresponds to the argumentality score of the complement based on a tf-idf measure (see below).

6.1 Description of our Approach

The starting point is a list of verbs along with their complements that have been automatically extracted from a large representative corpus. In our framework, a complement is a phrase directly connected to the verb (or is, in other words, a dependency of the verb), while the verb is the head of the dependents. In what follows we assume that complements are in fact couples made of a head noun and a dependency marker, generally a case marker.

6.1.1 Calculating the Argumenthood of Complements

Building on previous works [23, 24, 25, 26], Marchal [21, 1] proposes a new measure combining the prominent features describe in the literature. The measure is derived from the famous tf.idf used in information retrieval, with the major difference that we are dealing with complements instead of terms (or keywords), and with verbs instead of documents.

The proposed measure assigns a value between 0 and 1 to all the complements. 0 corresponds to a prototypical adjunct; 1 corresponds to a prototypical argument.

6.1.2 Minimal clustering at the verb entry level

Marchal [21, 1] introduces a method for merging verbal structures (i.e. a verb and a set of complements) into minimal predicate-frames structures using reliable lexical clues. He calls this technique *shallow clustering*. The technique is based on two principles: i) two verbal structures describing the same verb and having at least one common complement might correspond to the same verb meaning and ii) some complements are more informative than others for a given verb sense. The merging algorithm is presented at length in [21].

6.1.3 Modelling word senses through hierarchical clustering

Marchal [21, 1] proposes to cluster the minimal predicate-frames built during the *shallow clustering* procedure into a dendrogram structure. A dendrogram allows one to

define an arbitrary number of classes (using a threshold) and thus fit in with the goal
to model a continuum between ambiguity and vagueness. A dendrogram is usually
built using a hierarchical clustering algorithm and a distance matrix operating at the
input of the hierarchical clustering algorithm.

We must first define a vector representation for the minimal predicate-frames.
Following B. Partee and J. Mitchell, we suppose that "the meaning of a whole is a
function of the meaning of the parts and of the way they are syntactically combined"
[27]. Similarly we propose to calculate the meaning of the verb structure (i.e. the
construction) in function of the meaning of its parts. Following the principles of distributional semantics [28, 29] lexical heads can be represented in a vector space model
[30]. Case markers (or prepositions) can be used as syntactic information. Finally, we
propose to use our argumenthood measure to initialize the K parameter as it reflects
how important is a complement for a given verb.

Each verbal construction is transformed into a vector. The distance between two
vectors represents the dissimilarity between two occurrences of a same verb. Among
the very large number of metrics available to calculate the distance between two vectors, we chose the cosine similarity, since it is (as for the tf.idf score) simple, efficient
and perfectly suited to our problem.

Hierarchical clustering is an iterative process that clusters the two most similar
elements of a set into a single element and repeats the operation until there is only
one element left. Yet different clustering strategies are possible (*e.g.* single linkage,
complete linkage, average linkage). So as to select the best strategy (the one that will
preserve most of the information included in the distance matrix) we propose to apply
the cophenetic correlation coefficient. The details of this technique are presented in
[21, 1].

6.2 A visual interface to navigate the data

The major novelty of our approach is the description of predicative vocabulary of a
language (here verbs in Finnish) through a double continuum. In order to make the
resource usable by humans, it is necessary to develop a visual interface allowing the
end user to navigate the data and explore them in more details.

Our challenge is twofold: we want *i)* to produce a resource that reflects the sub-
tleties of continuous models but avoids the complexity of a multifactorial analysis
and *ii)* to offer a simple interface that allows a lexicographer or a linguist to navigate
easily the data collection. The goal is of course to make it possible for the end user to
discover interesting facts: new constructions, new idioms, and above all semantically
related linguistic sequences made of words that would otherwise (*i.e.* in isolation) not
be semantically related.

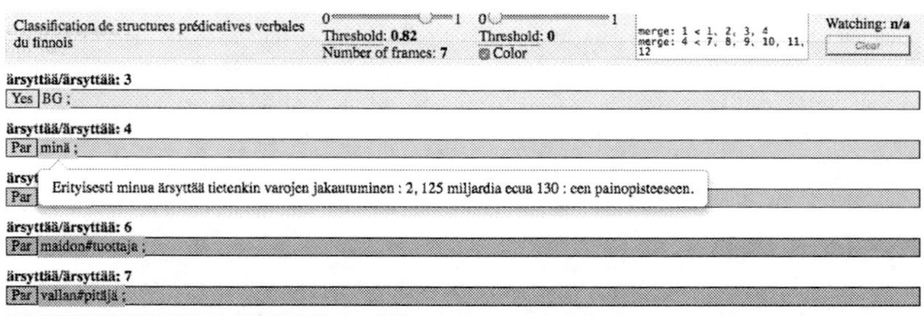

Figure 3: Web interface of the lexical acquisition system

After many attempts, we managed to propose a simple interface where the multifactorial analysis is abstracted as a double continuum: a continuum between ambiguity and vagueness [31], and a second continuum between arguments and adjuncts [25]. This double continuum is represented by two simple sliders.

Figure 3 shows a screen capture of our visualization tool. One can see two sliders on top of the interface: the first slider represents the continuum between ambiguity and vagueness (practically, this slider corresponds to a threshold in the dendrogram of the subentries; subentries with a distance inferior to the threshold are merged into a single subentry: when the threshold is set to 0, each minimal predicate-frame corresponds to a distinct subentry; when the threshold is set to 1 all minimal predicate-frames are merged into a single subentry). The second slider represents the continuum between arguments and adjuncts. It sets a threshold that selects complements that exhibit an argumenthood value greater than the threshold.

7   Conclusion

In this paper we have described some ongoing work on lexical acquisition for Finnish. The first application makes it possible to observe the partitive vs total object partition in this language. The second is a broader application aiming at acquiring a large database of verbal predicative structures in Finnish. The direct acquisition from a large corpus means that it is possible to get information on the use of verbs in context and also to collect statistics related to verb use. Statistics are especially important for nowadays applications based most of the time on a statistical approach.

The next stage consists in evaluating the results and checking their quality. This will in turn give us new perspectives to enhance the quality of the system, so as to take into account more linguistic features that are important for the task. We also plan to use a larger corpus soon (the Turku Dependency Treebank (TDT) [9]) so as to get more results for more verbs. Lastly, we plan to validate our data against a gold standard for Finnish so that lexical acquisition systems for this language can be compared.

Acknowledgments

This work has been mainly developed in the framework of the LAKME project. LAKME is funded by a grant from Paris Sciences et Lettres within the framework of the IDEX (Initiatives d'Excellence) PSL reference ANR-10- IDEX-0001- 02. The authors are also partially supported by a RGNF-CNRS (grant between the LATTICE-CNRS Laboratory and the Russian State University for the Humanities in Moscow).

References

[1] Pierre Marchal and Thierry Poibeau. A Continuum-based Model of Lexical Acquisition. In *CICLing Conference on Intelligent Text Processing and Computational Linguistics*, Konya, Turkey, 2016.

[2] Eugene Charniak. Immediate-head parsing for language models. In *Proceedings of the 39th Annual Meeting on Association for Computational Linguistics (ACL '01)*, pages 124–131, Toulouse, France, 2001.

[3] Dan Klein and Christopher D. Manning. Accurate unlexicalized parsing. In *Proceedings of the 41st Annual Meeting on Association for Computational Linguistics - Volume 1 (ACL '03)*, pages 423–430, Sapporo, Japan, 2003.

[4] Judita Preiss, Ted Briscoe, and Anna Korhonen. A system for large-scale acquisition of verbal, nominal and adjectival subcategorization frames from corpora. In *Proceedings of the 45th Meeting of the Association for Computational Linguistics (ACL'07)*, pages 912–918, Prague, Czech Rep., 2007.

[5] Cédric Messiant, Thierry Poibeau, and Anna Korhonen. Lexschem: a large subcategorization lexicon for french verbs. In *Proceedings of the International Conference on Language Resources and Evaluation (LREC'08)*, Marrakech, Morocco, 2008.

[6] Karin Kipper, Anna Korhonen, Neville Ryant, and Martha Palmer. Extending verbnet with novel verb classes. In *Proceedings of the Fifth International Conference on Language Resources and Evaluation (LREC-2006)*, Genoa, Italy, May 2006.

[7] Cédric Messiant, Kata Gábor, and Thierry Poibeau. Lexical acquisition from corpora: the case of subcategorization frames in french. *Traitement Automatique des Langues*, 51(1):65–96, 2010.

[8] Beth Levin. *English Verb Classes and Alternations: a preliminary investigation.* University of Chicago Press, Chicago and London, 1993.

[9] Katri Haverinen, Jenna Nyblom, Timo Viljanen, Veronika Laippala, Samuel Kohonen, Anna Missilä, Stina Ojala, Tapio Salakoski, and Filip Ginter. Building the essential resources for finnish: the turku dependency treebank. *Language Resources and Evaluation*, 48(3):493–531, 2014.

[10] Christopher D. Manning. Automatic acquisition of a large subcategorization dictionary from corpora. In *Proceedings of the 31st Meeting of the Association for Computational Linguistics (ACL'93)*, pages 235–242, Columbus, Ohio, USA, 1993.

[11] Michael R. Brent. From grammar to lexicon: Unsupervised learning of lexical syntax. *Computational Linguistics*, 19:203–222, 1993.

[12] Ted Briscoe and John Carroll. Automatic extraction of subcategorization from corpora. In *Proceedings of the 5th ACL Conference on Applied Natural Language Processing (ANLP)*, pages 356–363, Washington, DC., USA, 1997.

[13] Anna Korhonen. *Subcategorization acquisition.* PhD thesis, University of Cambridge, 2002.

[14] Anna Korhonen and Ted Briscoe. Extended lexical-semantic classification of english verbs. In Dan Moldovan and Roxana Girju, editors, *Proceedings of the HLT-NAACL Workshop on Computational Lexical Semantics*, pages 38–45, Boston, Massachusetts, USA, 2004.

[15] Sabine Schulte im Walde and Stefan Müller. Using web corpora for the automatic acquisition of lexical-semantic knowledge. *Journal for Language Technology and Computational Linguistics*, 28(2):85–105, 2013.

[16] Xiwu Han, Tiejun Zhao, Haoliang Qi, and Hao Yu. Subcategorization acquisition and evaluation for chinese verbs. In *Proceedings of the 20th International Conference on Computational Linguistics (COLING '04)*, Geneva, Switzerland, 2004.

[17] Fred Karlsson. *Finnish: An Essential Grammar.* 2nd ed, Routledge Essential Grammars, London, 2008.

[18] Bernd Bohnet, Joakim Nivre, Igor Boguslavsky, Richard Farkas, Filip Ginter, and Jan Hajic. Joint morphological and syntactic analysis for richly inflected languages. *Transactions of the Association for Computational Linguistics*, 1(4):415–428, 2013.

[19] Marie Catherine De Marneffe and Chris Manning. Stanford typed dependencies manual. *Technical report, Stanford University*, 2008.

[20] Marie Catherine De Marneffe and Chris Manning. Stanford typed dependencies representationl. *Technical report, Stanford University*, 2008.

[21] Pierre Marchal. *Acquisition de schémas prédicatifs verbaux en japonais.* PhD Thesis, INaLCO, 2015.

[22] Pierre Marchal and Thierry Poibeau. Lexical Knowledge Acquisition: Towards a Continuous and Flexible Representation of the Lexicon. In *Workshop IJCAI-Cognitum*, New York, 2016.

[23] Paola Merlo and Eva Esteve Ferrer. The notion of argument in prepositional phrase attachment. *Computational Linguistics*, 32(3):341–377, 2006.

[24] Omri Abend and Ari Rappoport. Fully unsupervised core-adjunct argument classification. In *Proceedings of the 48th Annual Meeting of the Association for Computational Linguistics (ACL'2010)*, pages 226–236, 2010.

[25] Christopher D. Manning. Probabilistic syntax. In S. Jannedy R. Bod, J. Hay, editor, *Probabilistic Linguistics*, pages 289–341. MIT Press, 2003.

[26] Cécile Fabre and Cécile Frérot. Groupes prépositionnels arguments ou circonstants : vers un repérage automatique en corpus. In *Actes de la 9è^{me} conférence sur le Traitement Automatique des Langues Naturelles (TALN 2002)*, pages 215–224, 2002.

[27] Barbara H. Partee. Lexical semantics and compositionality. In Lila R. Gleitman and Mark Liberman, editors, *An invitation to cognitive science. Volume 1: Language*, pages 311–360, Cambridge, MA, 1995. The MIT Press.

[28] J.R. Firth. A synopsis of linguistic theory (1930-1955). *Studies in linguistic analysis*, pages 1–32, 1957.

[29] Zellig S. Harris. Distributional structure. *Word*, 10:146–162, 1954.

[30] Grard Salton, Chung-Shu Yang, and Anita Wong. A vector space model for automatic indexing. *Communications of the ACM*, 18(11):613–620, 1975.

[31] David Tuggy. Ambiguity, polysemy, and vagueness. *Cognitive Linguistics*, 4(3):273–290, 1993.

Language technology resources and tools for Mansi: an overview

Csilla Horváth[1], Norbert Szilágyi[2], Veronika Vincze[3], Ágoston Nagy[2]
[1]University of Szeged, Institute of English-American Studies
cshorvath@ieas-szeged.hu, nagyagoston@yahoo.com
[2]University of Szeged, Department of Finno-Ugric Studies
norbertszilagyi91@gmail.com
[3]University of Szeged, Department of Informatics
vinczev@inf.u-szeged.hu

Abstract

In this paper, we offer an overview of language technology tools and resources (being) developed for an endangered minority language, Mansi. We pay special attention to lexical resources and morphological analyzers. Online dictionaries, morphological analyzers and a corpus are already available (or will be made available soon) for the language, which are described in the paper. Moreover, we also briefly present our efforts to contribute to the field of Mansi language technology. In several cases the weaknesses of existing resources or tools motivated us to implement some new tools, which are also presented in the paper. All of the tools and resources developed by us will be made freely available for the research community and anyone interested.

1   Introduction

According to a UNESCO review (UNESCO 2003) 50-90% of the known languages on Earth are likely to become extinct by the end of the century, thus any research on the unobserved aspects of endangered languages requires no further justification. Besides the importance of language documentation, the necessity of sociolinguistic or

The 3rd International Workshop for Computational Linguistics of Uralic Languages, pages 56–65,
St. Petersburg, Russia, 23–24 January 2017. ©2017 Association for Computational Linguistics

anthropological linguistic research as well as creating tools for language users and language learners is unquestionable.

The urbanization of indigenous people of Siberia has rarely been studied from a linguistic, ethnographic or cultural anthropological viewpoint, which calls for immediate reaction as excluding cities from fieldwork may often result in neglecting the majority of the Siberian population. This is especially true for people belonging to minorities in Russia: as for Obi-Ugric people, about a half of them cannot participate in linguistic and ethnographic studies [1]. Hence, sociolinguistic research of the Mansi language, especially revitalization efforts and the usage of urban language is of utmost importance.

In this paper, we aim at offering a landscape of language technology resources and tools for an endangered minority language, Mansi. Mansi (former term: Vogul) is an extremely endangered indigenous Uralic (more precisely Finno-Ugric, Ugric, Ob-Ugric) language, in minority position, spoken in Western Siberia, especially on the territory of the Khanty-Mansi Autonomous Okrug. Among the approximately 13,000 people who declared to be ethnic Mansi according to the data of the latest Russian federal census in 2010 only 938 stated that they could speak the Mansi language, which shows drastic decrease compared with the 2002 census figures (2,746 speakers).

The Mansi have been traditionally living on hunting, fishing, to a lesser extent also on reindeer breeding, they got acquainted with agriculture and urban lifestyle basically during the Soviet period. Urban lifestyle gained prominent importance in the last decades, the proportion of Mansis living in large villages, towns and cities has been constantly growing and by 2010 exceeded half of the Mansi population (57%). This tendency together with the unsatisfactory access to Mansi education and the weakening intergenerational transmission of the language makes the situation of Mansi vulnerable. Besides their scientific and academic novelty, the vulnerability of Mansi language also underlines the importance of creating computational tools for Mansi, for the benefit of scholars and researchers as well as language learners and language users.

The principles of Soviet linguistic policy according to which the Mansi literary language has been designed kept changing from time to time. After using Latin transcription for a short period, Mansi language planners had to switch to the Cyrillic transcription in 1937. While until the 1950s the more general tendency was to create new Mansi words to describe the formerly unknown phenomena, later on the usage of Russian loanwords became more dominant. Since the 1990s the tendencies governing the planning of Mansi language use and language acquisition have become multidimensional, important differences and interferences may be observed between the different actors of language use, especially the leading specialists (mainly following the Soviet academic policy) and the journalists (using and promoting the language on a daily basis, with the largest active number of followers). During our work we try to take every approach into consideration, when it is impossible to compromise (e.g. questions related to orthography), we tend to follow the examples found in majority language use.

In this paper, we aim at summarizing the current situation of Mansi within computational linguistics: we give a summary of the existing tools and resources (with special regard to lexical resources and morphological analyzers) and we will also briefly present our efforts to contribute to the field.

2 Lexical resources

2.1 Online dictionaries for Mansi

There are only a handful of dictionaries available for Mansi. The vocabularies collected by the early researchers of Mansi, Munkácsi's and Kannisto's (published as late as [2] and [3]) serve as great contribution and unfailing source of data for researchers. Nonetheless, they are inadequate for creating computational tools that would be equally useful for researchers and Mansi language users as well, partly because both dictionaries use especially detailed Latin-based script with plenty of diacritics, and partly because both dictionaries incorporate materials of different dialects and subdialects that have become extinct since the days of Munkácsi's and Kannisto's fieldworks. We are also aware of one small dictionary for Mansi (available at `http://glosbe.com/mns`), though this resource is limited in size as it is based on about 200 translated sentences, moreover, it applies Cyrillic and Latin transcriptions inconsistently.

Thus, instead of starting from the larger dictionaries compiled by European researchers, we decided to begin our work with the smaller, but more actively used dictionaries published by Mansi researchers, that is the Mansi-Russian-Mansi dictionary by Rombandeeva and Kuzakova (4,000 entries) [4] and the Russian-Mansi dictionary by Rombandeeva (11,000 entries) [5]. These dictionaries use Cyrillic script, contain most of the currently used Mansi vocabulary, and are often consulted by native Mansi or specialists working with the Mansi language and they are widely used in Mansi education.

The process of dictionary building is the following: the automatic optical character recognition is followed by manual correction and translation of the entries, and then this database is turned into a searchable, digitized dictionary [6], as detailed below.

The beta version of the online Mansi dictionary now contains approximately 20,000 entries[1]. The Mansi forms were retrieved from the PDF versions of Rombandeeva's and Kuzakova's [4], as well as Rombandeeva's [5] dictionaries by means of optical character recognition, then lexical entries from different sources were merged. It was also noted which dictionary and which page they come from. Translations that included several synonyms were added as separate items. The Mansi lexemes are supplemented with the Russian translation given by the dictionaries, and Hungarian (complete) and English (in progress) translations provided by linguists of the FinugRevita research group, parts of speech and annotation of the sources, i.e. the dictionaries that are contained within. In addition, information about their morphological paradigm is also encoded, as well as the argument structure of certain verbs.

The online Mansi dictionary being a key resource for creating a morphological analyzer, the project also aims to make it available for public use as well, thus meeting a long-felt need for a sufficient Mansi–English–Mansi and a suitable online Mansi dictionary. After some technical refinements, our online Mansi dictionary will be made available on the Giellatekno website (http://giellatekno.uit.no).

We also plan to collate our dictionary with the data on the Northern Mansi dialect group of Munkácsi's enormous Mansi–Hungarian dictionary [2] – by relying on its simplified transcipt by Béla K'almán – and also expand it with the Northern Mansi material of Balandin's and Vakhrusheva's Mansi–Russian dictionary [7], as well as with dozens of the most necessary neologisms describing different features of contemporary lifestyle (such as the urban environment, oil mining or judicial terms), created and used first and foremost by the journalists of the Mansi newspaper *Luima Seripos* (see below).

2.2 Mansi Wordnet

Recently, another lexical resource has been constructed for Mansi: [8] report on the construction of a wordnet for Mansi. Special challenges were met during the building process, among which the most important ones are the low number of native speakers, the lack of thesauri and the bear language. The bear is a prominently sacred animal venerated by Mansi, thus triggering a detailed taboo language. Since the bear is thought to understand the human speech, it is required to use taboo words while speaking about the bear, the parts of its body, or any activity connected with the bear (especially bear hunting) so that the bear would not understand it. Thus vocabulary items belonging to the bear language had to be separately indicated in the Mansi wordnet, which currently contains about 300 synsets and is under constant

---

[1]Note that the number of the entries exceeds the sum of the entries of the individual ditionaries. This is due to synonyms and different senses of Mansi words, which were grouped under the same head entry in the Russian–Mansi dictionary, but are now counted separately.

development. As for the proportion of part-of-speech categories, nouns prevail over
verbs with 210 nouns (70%) and 90 verbs.

3 Mansi Morphological Analyzers

Mansi is a morphologically rich language, similar to other Uralic languages. Thus,
its automatic morphological processing requires a properly designed morphological
analyzer. For Mansi, there already exists a morphological analyzer [9] developed by
MorphoLogic Ltd.[2]. However, this has several issues that are problematic concerning
contemporary Mansi language use. First, it employs Latin-based transcription used
by scholars but the Mansi orthography used by the speakers themselves is Cyrillic-
based. Second, its vocabulary is based on Munkácsi's Mansi dictionary [2] and it was
optimized for the texts covered in Kálmán's *Chrestomathia Vogulica* [10] and *Wogulische Texte* [11], mostly collected at the end of the 19th and the first half of the 20th
century. Hence, the contemporary lexicon and genres of the 20th and 21st centuries
are underrepresented. Third, it is not open-source.

For all the above mentioned reasons, we chose to create a new morphological analyzer for Mansi from scratch. From among the many currently available finite-state
tools, the HFST standard was chosen in order that the analyzer could be integrated
into the framework which is used at the GiellaTekno website. This choice is thus motivated by the fact that in this way, the morphological analyzer can be integrated into
a large system dealing with minority languages with a common interface. The files
in the morphological analyzer can be grouped into two categories: stems and affixes.
Mansi words (stems) are given in a lexicon, together with morphological information
and their Russian translations, in addition, there are morphological rules that are re-
sponsible for analyzing and generating different inflectional forms of the individual
stems. Furthermore, stems and affixes are organized into different files on the basis
of their part-of-speech category, since nouns are conjugated differently than verbs,
and the whole system is easier to modify and to look through.

The dictionary mentioned in Section 2.1 serves as a basis for the lexicon integrated
into the morphological analyzer. Nevertheless, the original paper-based dictionaries
were published decades ago, which means that the lexicon cannot contain contemporary terms of vocabulary (e.g. those related to internet and social media). Thus, it
is constantly expanded by adding novel lexical items in a semi-automatic way: the
analyzer is regularly run on contemporary texts and if some of the words cannot get
a proper morphological analysis, their stem is added to the lexicon.

---

[2]http://www.morphologic.hu/urali/index.php?lang=hungarian&a_lang=chv

Another issue with stems is that multiword items were extremely frequent in the dictionaries. For example, the учитель 'schoolteacher *masc.*' could be translated as няврамыт ханисьтан хум built up of the element *children-teaching man* , and the feminine counterpart учительница 'schoolteacher *fem.*' as няврамыт ханисьтан нэ from *children-teaching woman.* However, the HFST formalism could not support multiword items and they needed to be reduced to their syntactic head, in this case, хум and нэ.

As for the morphological rules, lexical entries of Mansi were grouped into different morphological categories depending on the inflectional paradigm they belong to. For this, we relied on the descriptions found in several Mansi grammars [12, 13], as well as on the linguistic intuitions of native speakers of Mansi.

In order to classify the Mansi stems into inflectional paradigms, we analyzed the words' phonological structure. First, we listed all the possible syllables that can occur at the beginning of the word, at the end of the word, or within words. This was an important step in establishing inflectional paradigms as in the case of nouns, it is the last (two) syllable(s) that determine the quality of affixes and linking vowels, whereas in the case of verbs, it is the number of syllables and the quality of the last syllable. Then, inflectional paradigms were created for each type separately in order to be able to analyze and generate all inflectional forms of Mansi nouns and verbs. Right now, the system includes 36 nominal and 27 verbal paradigms.

Here we offer a short sample of the nominal stems and inflectional paradigms for illustrative purposes. The first column denotes the stem and its inflectional stem. The second column contains the inflectional paradigm it belongs to, e.g. N_CVS_masnut__n means that it is a nominal paradigm for nouns that end in a combination of a vowel and a softening consonant, a typical example of which is *masnut* 'cloth'.

```
миркол:миркол      N_CVS_masnut__n     "сельсовет" ;
щёмья:щёмья        N_VO_maa__n         "семья" ;
нэпак:нэпак        N_CVH_luw__n        "книга" ;
ӯльпа:ӯльпа        N_VO_maa__n         "кедр" ;

LEXICON N_VO_maa__n
N_VO_maa__n ;

! non possessive forms

+N+Sg+Nom: K ;
+N+Sg+Loc:т K ;
+N+Sg+Lat:н K ;
```

+N+Sg+Abl:ныл K ;
+N+Sg+Ins:л K ;
+N+Sg+Tra:г K ;

+N+Du+Nom:г K ;
+N+Du+Loc:гт K ;
+N+Du+Lat:гн K ;
+N+Du+Abl:гныл K ;
+N+Du+Ins:гтыл K ;

+N+Pl+Nom:т K ;
+N+Pl+Loc:тт K ;
+N+Pl+Lat:тн K ;
+N+Pl+Abl:тныл K ;
+N+Pl+Ins:тыл K ;

Based on the above information, the following morphological analyses are provided by the system for the word щёмьят "families" or "in family":

    щёмьят щёмья+N+Pl+Nom
    щёмьят щёмья+N+Sg+Loc

Beside parts-of-speech that can be inflected, the morphological analyzer also includes words belonging to parts-of-speech that cannot be inflected. For instance, adverbs, conjunctions and interjections are also adequately recognized by the system.

Our Mansi morphological analyzer will be made freely available soon within the Giellatekno infrastructure.

4   Mansi corpora

In order to test our morphological tools, we have started to create a Mansi corpus, which consists of the articles published in the Mansi newspaper *Luima Seripos* (Mansi for "Northern dawn"). The online archive of *Luima Seripos* is available on the homepage of the joint editorial board of *Luima Seripos* and regional Khanty newspaper *Khanty Yasang*.[3]. The Mansi texts published in *Luima Seripos* cover various topics

---

[3] `http://www.khanty-yasang.ru/luima-seripos/archive`

such as traditional lifestyle, folklore and short biographies, as well as domains of urban life.

Currently, the corpus contains issues of *Luima Seripos* from 2013 (more precisely, issues 1050-1131). The corpus consists of 520,000 tokens, converted into XML format. Cyrillic characters with diacritics, i.e. those that denote vowel length were segmented into two characters: the vowel itself and the macron, which enables a proper display of the Unicode characters (the original website is sometimes inadequaly displayed on certain machines or browsers). We have been constantly working on the extension of the corpus and we are planning to add about 150,000 tokens to it.

The following metadata are also assigned to the texts of the corpus: number of issue, date of publication, author of the article, title of the article, link to the article and a unique identifier for each article within the corpus. Also, the XML file applies special tags for named entities such as person names and locations as well as embedded texts written in Russian.

As work in progress, we would like to mention that about 5,000 tokens of the corpus are being manually annotated for part-of-speech tags and syntactic structures so that later on we can test and evaluate our morphological analyzer and POS tagger under development.

5   Conclusions

In this paper, we offered an overview of language technology tools and resources (being) developed for Mansi. Online dictionaries, morphological analyzers and a corpus are already available (or will be made available soon) for the language, however, there is still room for improvement. In addition to the constant update and extension of the above mentioned tools, we intend to create a small dependency treebank of Mansi in harmony with the Universal Dependencies project [14], which may enhance the implementation of a syntactic parser for Mansi. To reach the widest possible range of active users we consider the opportunity of creating online games based on the already existing computational tools. For the Mansi language users and language learners we plan to produce online games activating the users knowledge on Mansi vocabulary. We intend to make all of our resources and tools freely available to anyone interested.

The majority of the future Mansi audience of computational language tools, such as children, teenagers and young adults were raised in multiethnic families and multiculticultural settlements, most of the cases in towns and cities. Only 0.72% of the total population of the Khanty–Mansi Autonomous Okrug belongs to Mansi ethnicity, this proportion occasionally may be higher in cities, as for example in the capital of the Okrug, Khanty–Mansiysk (1.5%). This condition together with the weakening intergenerational transmission of the language and the just gradually changing educational system make the situation of Mansi vulnerable. The young Mansi language users and language learners are familiar with the newest technological developments, in general they have internet access and use the social media as well, most of them got acquainted with computational language teaching tools as well in alternative educational institutions [15]. Thus, besides their scientific and academic novelty, the creation of computational tools for the Mansi language is crucial for the benefit of the language learners and language users as well.

Acknowledgments

This work was supported in part by the Finnish Academy of Sciences and the Hungarian National Research Fund, within the framework of the project *Computational tools for the revitalization of endangered Finno-Ugric minority languages (FinUgRevita)*. Project number: OTKA FNN 107883; AKA 267097.

References

[1] Z. Nagy. Szibéria néprajza és a város: Akik kimaradtak az összefoglalókból. In S. Szeverényi and T. Szécsényi, editors, *Érdekes nyelvészet*, 2016.

[2] B. Munkácsi and B. Kálmán. *Wogulisches Wörterbuch*. Akadémiai Kiadó, Budapest, 1986.

[3] Artturi Kannisto. *Wogulisches Wörterbuch*. Helsinki, 2013. Kotimaisten Kielten Keskuksen Julkaisuja 173.

[4] Е. И. Ромбандеева and Е. А. Кузакова. *Словарь мансийско-русский и русско-мансийский*. Просвещение, Ленинград, 1982.

[5] Е. И. Ромбандеева. *Русско-мансийский словарт*. Миралл, Санкт-Петербург, 2005.

[6] N. Thieberger and A. L. Berez. Linguistic Data Management. In N. Thieberger, editor, *The Oxford Handbook of Linguistic Fieldwork*, chapter 4, pages 90–118. Oxford University Press, Oxford, 2012.

[7] А. Н. Баландин and М. П. Вахрушева. *Мансийско-русский словарь с лексическими паралеллями из южно-мансийского (кондинского) диалекта*. Просвещение, Ленинград, 1958.

[8] Csilla Horváth, Ágoston Nagy, Norbert Szilágyi, and Veronika Vincze. Where Bears Have the Eyes of Currant: Towards a Mansi WordNet. In Verginica Barbu Mititelu, Corina Forascu, Christiane Fellbaum, and Piek Vossen, editors, *Proceedings of the Eighth Global WordNet Conference*, pages 130–134, Bucuresti, Romania, 2016.

[9] Gábor Prószéky. Endangered Uralic Languages and Language Technologies. In *Proceedings of the Workshop on Language Technologies for Digital Humanities and Cultural Heritage*, pages 1–2, Hissar, Bulgaria, September 2011.

[10] B. Kálmán. *Chrestomathia Vogulica*. Tankönyvkiadó, Budapest, 1963.

[11] Béla Kálmán. *Wogulische Texte mit einem Glossar*. Akadémiai Kiadó, Budapest, 1976.

[12] T. Riese. *Vogul*. Number 158 in Languages of the World/Materials. Lincom Europa, München - New Castle, 2001.

[13] Е. И. Ромбандеева. *Мансийский (вогульский) язык*. Наука, Москва, 1973.

[14] Joakim Nivre, Marie-Catherine de Marneffe, Filip Ginter, Yoav Goldberg, Jan Hajic, Christopher D. Manning, Ryan McDonald, Slav Petrov, Sampo Pyysalo, Natalia Silveira, Reut Tsarfaty, and Daniel Zeman. Universal Dependencies v1: A Multilingual Treebank Collection. In *Proceedings of the Tenth International Conference on Language Resources and Evaluation (LREC 2016)*, 2016.

[15] Csilla Horváth. Old problems and new solution: Teaching methods in the governmental and alternative Mansi educational institutions. *Finnisch-Ugrische Mitteilungen*, 39:37–48, 2013.

Annotation schemes in North Sámi dependency parsing

Mariya Sheyanova
Fundamental and Applied Linguistics
Higher School of Economics
Moscow, Russia
masha.shejanova@gmail.com

Francis M. Tyers
Giela ja kultuvrra instituhtta
UiT Norgga árktalaš universitehta
N-9018 Romsa, Norway
francis.tyers@uit.no

Abstract

In this paper we describe a comparison of two annotation schemes for dependency parsing of North Sámi, a Finno-Ugric language spoken in the north of Scandinavia and Finland. The two annotation schemes are the Giellatekno (GT) scheme which has been used in research and applications for the Sámi languages and Universal Dependencies (UD) which is a cross-lingual scheme aiming to unify annotation stations across languages. We show that we are able to deterministically convert from the Giellatekno scheme to the Universal Dependencies scheme without a loss of parsing performance. While we do not claim that either scheme is *a priori* a more adequate model of North Sámi syntax, we do argue that the choice of annotation scheme is dependent on the intended application.

The 3rd International Workshop for Computational Linguistics of Uralic Languages, pages 66–75,
St. Petersburg, Russia, 23–24 January 2017. ©2017 Association for Computational Linguistics

1   Introduction

Dependency parsing is an important step in many applications of natural language processing, such as information extraction, machine translation, interactive language learning and corpus search interfaces. There are a number of approaches to dependency parsing. These include rule-based approaches such as [1] for German and [2] for Portuguese, and statistical approaches, such as transition-based parsing, exemplified by MaltParser [3]. In rule-based approaches the knowledge source is a set of rules (such as constraints), while in statistical approaches the knowledge source is a collection of parsed sentences called *treebank*.

Both rule-based and statistical approaches have in common that the parses they output conform to a given annotation scheme, that is a set of rules which define what linguistic structure should be applied to given constructions. Annotation schemes can vary substantially according to how they encode an analysis of linguistic structure. For example, one scheme may decide that the auxiliary verb is the head of an auxiliary—main verb construction because of subject agreement, while another may decide that the main verb is the head because of case government of arguments.

The choice of representation can depend heavily on application. For certain applications, such as grammar checking, a more morphosyntactic scheme may be appropriate, while for others, such as machine translation, a more syntacto-semantic scheme may be more appropriate.

In this paper, we describe the conversion of the annotation schemes output by the Giellatekno parser to a corresponding UD-compliant scheme. We also provide comparative statistics on the composition of the corpus used in the experiments before and after the conversion. Afterwards, we report a comparison of parsing results using the two annotation schemes. The paper is structured as follows: Section 2 describes the corpus and source annotation scheme used in this paper; section 3 describes the conversion procedure and the target annotation scheme; section 4 describes an experiment in comparing annotation schemes and finally section 5 presents some concluding remarks.

2   Corpus

The corpus is a collection of sentences in North Sámi from a variety of genres (literature, news, religion, grammar examples) which have been manually disambiguated and annotated for shallow syntactic function. There are a total of 3,682 sentences comprising 35,061 tokens. In order to produce a treebank, this disambiguated corpus was processed with a rule-based parser, as described below.

2.1 Rule-based parser

Giellatekno's rule-based dependency parser [4] is based on the VISL Constraint Grammar formalism [5]. The parser consists of 394 rules, of which 242 are head-assignment rules in the form "set the head of token t to the head matched by the pattern p", and 152 are label-assignment rules in the form "set the label of token t to l in context c". The following two examples illustrate these rule types.

```
SETPARENT @SUBJ TO (*1 VFIN)
```
  Set the head of a token with the function subject to the finite verb to the right

```
SUBSTITUTE (@FMV) (@FS-<SUBJ) TARGET V (-1 SPRED) (0 Qst)
```
  A finite-main verb is a clausal subject if there is a previous predicate
  and the current verb has a question marker

The parser is designed to be run as the last stage of a pipeline that consists of finite-state morphological analysis and constraint-grammar-based morphological disambiguation and shallow-function labelling. The same parser is used for other Sámi languages, such as Lule Sámi and South Sámi and has also been applied to parsing South Sámi, Faroese and Greenlandic. The parser has an F-score of 0.99 for North Sámi [4], but in practice this may be lower (see section 3.2 for details).

2.2 Annotation scheme

The dependency structure produced by the parser is a compromise between Sámi grammatical tradition and the conventions used in the VISL project [2]. The core distinctions in the scheme for verbs are: finite versus non-finite verbs, main verbs versus auxiliary verbs, and main clauses versus subordinate clauses. For nominal modifiers, the core distinction is the part-of-speech category of the head.

For verb complexes (i.e. a main verb along with any auxiliary or modal verbs), the annotation scheme follows the chained analysis, where the finite auxiliary is the head subsequent verbs are chained according to government. This analysis also applies to the negative verb, which is head when it is finite.

In co-ordination, the first conjunct is the head and subsequent conjuncts attach to the first conjunct. Conjunctions attach to their immediately preceding conjunct, and the dependency relation for each conjunct is the same as the head. There is a distinction between local conjunction (for example between modifiers) and global conjunction (between finite-verb clauses).

North Sámi has both prepositions and postpositions, in both cases the adposition is the head of adpositional phrase, and the head of the noun-phrase complement is

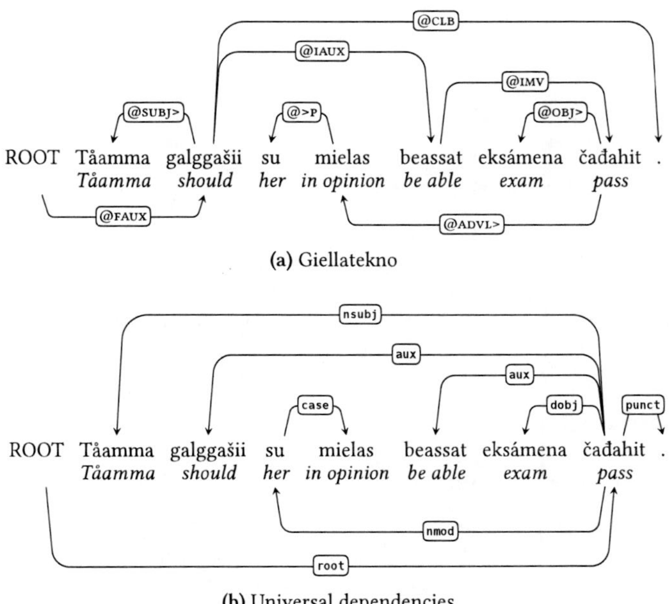

(a) Giellatekno

(b) Universal dependencies

Figure 1: Two structures for the sentence *Tåamma galggašii su mielas beassat eksámena čađahit.* 'Tåamma should in her opinion be able to pass the exam.' which illustrate different principles behind the two annotation schemes in head assignment and labels. Note that the Giellatekno annotation contains a non-projective dependency between *čađahit* 'to pass' and *mielas* 'in the opinion of'.

the dependent. For numeral phrases, if the numeral takes the case of its function, e.g. object in accusative and the nominal is in the genitive (2a), then the numeral is head, while if the numeral agrees with the nominal or is in the attributive form then the nominal is head (2b).

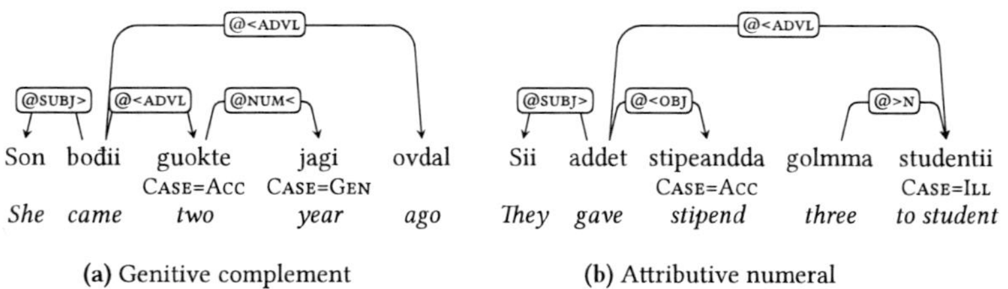

(a) Genitive complement   (b) Attributive numeral

Figure 2: Annotation of numeral phrases in the Giellatekno scheme

Throughout the article we use the convention of prefixing an @ symbol to dependency labels using the Giellatekno scheme, labels without the @ are Universal dependency labels.

3 Conversion

3.1 Universal dependencies

Universal Dependencies [6] is an international collaborative project to make cross-linguistically consistent treebanks available for a wide variety of languages. In the UD annotation scheme, to improve cross-linguistic compatibility, dependency relations are primarily between content words, with function words attaching as leaf nodes. The motivation for this is that content words are more stable between languages, while languages can vary with how e.g. cases are used as opposed to adpositions, and analytic versus synthetic tense constructions. Thus, in auxiliary–main verb constructions, the main verb is the head and the auxiliary is attached as a dependent, if there is more than one auxiliary they are attached as siblings as opposed to a nested structure. In adpositional phrases, the complement of the adposition is the head and the adposition itself is a dependent attached with the case relation.

In terms of label categories, in contrast to the Giellatekno scheme where labels for non-verbal modifiers indicate the part of speech of the head of the relation, in the UD scheme, labels indicate the part-of-speech of the modifier. For example a noun phrase or adpositional phrase receives the label nmod 'nominal modifier', while an

Rule type	Count
$a \rightarrow b$	12
$a \rightarrow b$ with context	47
$a \rightarrow b$ with tree context	11
$a \rightarrow b$ with tree transformation	16
Total:	86

Table 1: Statistics on rule-types. $a \rightarrow b$ denotes that the rules change GT label a to UD label b. There was one additional rule which performed a tree transformation with no relabelling operation to reattach punctuation.

adjective modifying a nominal has the relation amod 'adjectival modifier'. Like in the Giellatekno scheme, a distinction is made between core arguments (subject, object, complement clause) and obliques (such as adverbials).

3.2 Preprocessing

An important step in the conversion process is the removal of sentences for which the rule-based parser produces a malformed tree. We count as malformed those trees which either: (a) have more than one node attaching to the technical root, (b) have cycles, (c) have no node attaching to the technical root, or (d) have orphan nodes, that is tokens which do not have a head. Out of a total of 3,682 sentences in the original corpus, 128 fall into class (b) or (d), 42 fall into class (a) and 8 fall into class (c). This leaves 3,504 sentences, or 30,955 tokens to be converted.

3.3 Rules

In order to convert from the Giellatekno annotation scheme to Universal dependencies, several types of transformations need to be carried out. The simplest are label replacements that do not require any context, for example replacing the Giellatekno label @FS-SUBJ with the UD label csubj. In this case we do not even need to look at the part-of-speech of the node as it is encoded in the label.

The second type are label replacements that require looking at other features of the node as context, for example to replace the Giellatekno label @>N we need to determine if the current token is a noun in genitive (in which case we output nmod:poss), a noun in a locative case (in which case we output nmod), an adjective (in which case we output amod), a demonstrative pronoun (in which case we output det).

The third type are label replacements that require looking at tree context but do not do any tree transformations, for example to convert the Giellatekno label @FMV, if the head is the technical root, then it is converted to root, if the head is a speech verb then we convert it to ccomp, if the head is another @FMV and there is no explicit coordinator then we convert it to parataxis.

The fourth type are rules that include both tree transformations (switching head-/dependent or moving nodes in the tree) and label substitutions. For example for adpositional phrases, the adposition is moved to be the dependent of the head nominal in the NP and label is changed to case. The label which attached the adposition to its head is retained and now is the relations between the head of the PP and the head noun.

All of the rules are implemented in XSLT [7], which is a declarative language for transforming XML trees. The transformations are run as a pipeline, with the output of one rule feeding as the input of the next. In general, rules are ordered by complexity with more complex transformation rules being run first. Table 1 gives a summary of the rule types and frequency of rule types. The transformation rules are available online.[1] In addition to the linguistic rules we also wrote a rule for reattaching punctuation in order to try and reduce the amount of non-projectivity.

3.4 Postprocessing

The rules described in section 3.3 may produce invalid trees, either as a result of an error in the output of the rule-based parser, or an error in the transformation rules.[2] We have tried to minimise the number of errors in the rules, but sometimes it might not be clear what the best course of action is. With regard to errors in the original parser output, one possibility would be to fix them manually before conversion or fix the rules, but this was not done in order to preserve reproducibility. Parser errors were however reported upstream to the authors of [4]. To remove invalid trees from the final output we ran the same validation scripts that were used to detect invalid trees in the input. After applying postprocessing we were left with 3,304 sentences, and 29,354 tokens. A summary of the statistics for the converted sentences can be found in Table 2

---

[1] https://github.com/ftyers/UD_North_Saami

[2] While the XSLT-based parser will not produce formally-invalid XML, because of the data format, which specifies linear order with an order attribute, it may produce trees where an order attribute points to a node that has been deleted.

	Giellatekno	Universal dependencies
Tokens	29,354	29,354
Sentences	3,304	3,304
Projective	2,596	2,927
Non-projective	708	377
Avg. distance from head	2.59	2.75
Relations	44	32
Relations (incl. direction)	58	32
Avg. labels/lemma	1.83	1.57

Table 2: Comparative statistics for the Giellatekno and UD annotation schemes. Relations (including direction) indicates the number of labels if head-direction indicators are taken into account.

4   Experiment

In order to test the utility of the two annotations schemes in a real-world setting, we trained and evaluated a number of models using the popular UDpipe toolkit [8]. UDpipe is a toolkit for data-driven tokenisation, part-of-speech tagging and dependency parsing; it learns a statistical model for each of the tasks from treebank data and applies this model to process unseen sentences.

We perform 10-fold cross-validation by randomising the order of sentences in the corpus and splitting them into 10 equally-sized parts. In each iteration we held out one part for testing and used the rest for training. We trained UDpipe for 10 epochs, the default setting. We calculated the labelled-attachment score (LAS) and unlabelled-attachment score (UAS) for each of the models. In addition to the LAS and UAS we also calculated the raw label accuracy. The same splits were used for both annotation schemes. Table 3 presents the results for each of the schemes.

Scheme	UAS	LAS	Labels
Giellatekno	[91.2, 93.4]	[88.8, 91.1]	[92.58, 94.83]
Universal dependencies	[78.2, 83.4]	[76.0, 80.9]	[78.00, 81.81]

Table 3: Results for parsing from the two annotation schemes, intervals are the high/low scores from 10-fold cross validation.

Despite the smaller label set, the UD annotation scheme performs worse than the GT scheme.

5 Concluding remarks

We have presented a comparison of two annotation schemes for dependency parsing of North Sámi. The labels and annotation guidelines in the Giellatekno scheme are closely coupled with Sámi morphosyntax, while the Universal dependencies scheme aims to be more cross-linguistically consistent. Preliminary results show that we are able to achieve better parsing performance using the Giellatekno annotation scheme, this is in contrast to other work such as [9] who find better results using Universal dependencies.

In terms of future work, we aim to convert the part-of-speech tags and features to UD-standard ones, and work with authors of the other Uralic treebanks to improve cross-linguistic compatibility. With the release of version 2.0 of the UD guidelines we also plan to convert update the rules to produce trees in line with the new guidelines. It is also our intention to investigate why the parsing performance is substantially worse for the UD-based representation, and to manually validate a proportion of the data to use as a gold standard in future experiments.

Acknowledgements

We are grateful to Trond Trosterud for help with the Giellatekno annotation scheme and to the reviewers for their helpful comments.

References

[1] I. Schröder, W. Menzel, K. Foth, and M. Schulz. "Modeling dependency grammar with restricted constraints". In: *Traitement Automatique des Langues* 41.1 (2000), pp. 113–144.

[2] E. Bick. "Turning Constraint Grammar Data into Running Dependency Treebanks". In: *Proceedings of the Fourth Workshop on Treebanks and Linguistic Theory, TLT4*. Ed. by M. Civit and S. Kübler. 2005.

[3] J. Nivre, J. Hall, J. Nilsson, A. Chanev, G. Eryiğit, S. Kübler, S. Marinov, and E. Marsi. "MaltParser: A language-independent system for data-driven dependency parsing". In: *Natural Language Engineering* 13.2 (2007), pp. 95–135.

[4] L. Antonsen, T. Trosterud, and L. Wiechetek. "Reusing Grammatical Resources for New Languages". In: *Proceedings of the Eighth International Conference on Language Resources and Evaluation (LREC'10)*. Malta: European Language Resources Association (ELRA), 2010.

[5] E. Bick and T. Didriksen. "CG-3 – Beyond Classical Constraint Grammar". In: *Proceedings of the 20th Nordic Conference of Computational Linguistics, NODAL-IDA 2015, May 11-13, 2015, Vilnius, Lithuania*. 109. Linköping University Electronic Press, Linköpings universitet, 2015, pp. 31–39.

[6] J. Nivre, M.-C. de Marneffe, F. Ginter, Y. Goldberg, J. Hajič, C. D. Manning, R. McDonald, S. Petrov, S. Pyysalo, N. Silveira, R. Tsarfaty, and D. Zeman. "Universal Dependencies v1: A Multilingual Treebank Collection". In: *Proceedings of the Tenth International Conference on Language Resources and Evaluation (LREC'16)*. 2016.

[7] J. Clark. *XSL Transformations (XSLT) Version 1.0*. World Wide Web Consortium, Recommendation REC-xslt-19991116. Nov. 1999.

[8] M. Straka, J. Hajič, and J. Straková. "UDPipe: Trainable Pipeline for Processing CoNLL-U Files Performing Tokenization, Morphological Analysis, POS Tagging and Parsing". In: *Proceedings of the Tenth International Conference on Language Resources and Evaluation (LREC'16)*. Portorož, Slovenia: European Language Resources Association (ELRA), May 2016. ISBN: 978-2-9517408-9-1.

[9] U. Sulubacak, M. Gökırmak, F. M. Tyers, Ç. Çöltekin, J. Nivre, and G. Eryiğit. "Universal dependencies for Turkish". In: *Proceedings of COLING 2016*. 2016.

A morphological analyser for Kven

Sindre Trosterud
Kainun institutti

Trond Trosterud
Giellatekno, UiT

Anna-Kaisa Räisänen
Kainun institutti

Leena Niiranen
UiT

Mervi Haavisto
Kainun institutti

Kaisa Maliniemi
Ruija kvenmuseum

Abstract

We present a morphological analyser for Kven, a Finnic language spoken in Northern Norway. Apart from the overall view of the analyser, we discuss principles for whether to treat morphological processes like gemination and stem-conditioned suffix variation as lexically, morphologically or phonologically conditioned alternations. The choice is often governed by the grammatical mechanism itself, but in many instances the analysis may be carried out in more than one way and it becomes a choice of where to place the complexity. The article discusses some of the choices we made in this particular case.

1 Introduction

The article presents a morphological analyser for the Kven language, i. e. a program that is an explicit model of the Kven grammar, by which the user may either analyse or generate any Kven wordform, and presents both program design choices and some of the usage possibilities.

The article is structured as follows: Section 2 first gives the technical background for the technologies used to create this analyser, and then an overview of the Kven language itself. Section 3 presents how we have implemented this FST, discusses the rationale behind some of our choices, describes our test setup and mentions the applications in which the analyser is used. In section 4 we evaluate the analyser, and section 5 contains a conclusion.

The 3rd International Workshop for Computational Linguistics of Uralic Languages, pages 76–88,
St. Petersburg, Russia, 23–24 January 2017. ©2017 Association for Computational Linguistics

2 Background

2.1 Theoretical background

This analyser is modeled like a finite-state transducer. A finite-state transducer (FST) is an automaton with both an input tape and an output tape, that defines relations between pairs of strings. When made as a specialized finite-state automation (a lexical transducer) it maps lexemes and morphological specifications (in the form of tags) to corresponding inflected forms, and vice versa.

The transducer modeling morphological processes for Kven actually consists of two separate transducers. The first one is a Lexicon Transducer (Morphological) that takes input A = {the lexeme and a string of tags denoting the grammatical analysis of the word form in question}, then the second one is a morphophonological transducer that uses the first transducer's output B = {the stem + trigger and suffixes} as input, and outputs C = {a string of letters, i.e. the word form}. The transducers are composed, so that $A/B * B/C = A/C$ (or in standard notation: $A : B$ .o. $B : C = A : C$). The transducer is bidirectional, and gives both analysis and generation.

```
A = t a k k i +N +Sg +Gen
B = t a k k i ^WG >  n

B = t a k k i ^WG > n
C = t a k 0 i 0   0 n
```

In practice (as shown above): the lexicon transducer is for concatenative morphology, pairing lexeme and grammatical tags to stem, suffixes and possible trigger symbols. The morphophonological is for global morphological processes like gemination, consonant gradation and vowel harmony.

A morphological transducer may be described as a set of paths running through the decision tree of all possible stems and affix combinations of the language, and combining lemma + analysis string with its corresponding word form. An ideal transducer for Kven will for a given token return all and only the valid analyses, and for a given analysis generate all and only the valid surface forms.

We built these two components of the Kven transducer using the Finite-State Lexicon Compiler (lexc) as the Lexicon Transducer and the Xerox Two-level Rule Compiler (twolc) as the morphophonological one ([2], [6]). The stems + conjugation are written in .lexc files grouped by word type where the stems are connected (pointed) to a specific sublexicon which contains the conjugational abstractions of a subset of a word group consisting of words acting similarly in the conjugations. This process creates what basically amounts to a decision tree of all possible realisations for all of the words added to the analyser.

The analyser is implemented in the Giellatekno & Divvun infrastructure created and maintained at UiT The Arctic University of Norway, cf. [9](`http://giellatekno.uit.no`).

2.2 The Kven language

The Kven language *(kväänin kieli)* is a Finnic language spoken by the Kven people in Northern Norway, primarily in the municipalities shown on the map[1] in Figure 1. The language and the Kvens have their historical roots in the areas that today are part of Northern Sweden and Northern Finland. The wave of Kven emigration towards the Norwegian coast continued for several hundred years beginning from the 16th century.

Figure 1: The main municipalities where Kven is spoken

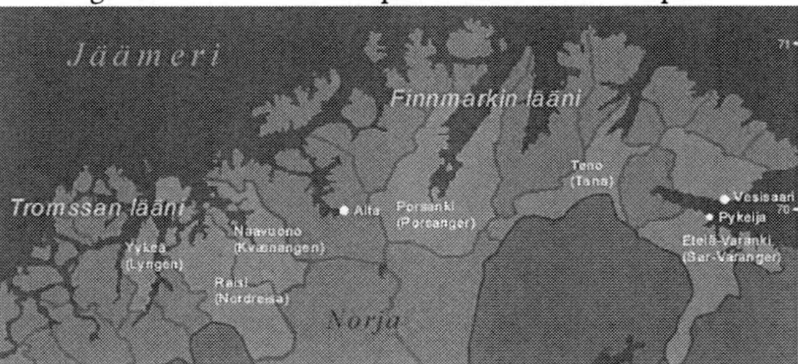

The Kven language is closely related to Meänkieli in Sweden and the Far Northern dialects of Finnish. However, the language differs from Meänkieli and Finnish dialects because of its separation from these languages e.g. through morphological innovations ([7]) and close contact with Norwegian and North Saami.

As a result of this Kven is a language phonologically very close to northern Finnish dialect, but with several morphological innovation. While sharing its basic vocabulary with Finnish and Meänkieli, Kven has not adapted the vocabulary created for standard Finnish in order to cope with the modern society, instead Kven has borrowed from Norwegian, and to a limited extent also from North Saami. As a result,

---

[1]The map was made by Alphaios at Wikimedia Commons.

a Finn understanding Finnish dialects and Scandinavian will understand Kven, but a Kven speaker will have greater problems understanding standard Finnish.

Kven is an agglutinative language, which means that to express tense, mood, number, and person, affixes are attached to the word stem. Kven has acquired many loan words not only from Norwegian and Swedish but also from the Saami languages. Many Swedish and Saami loan words already belonged to the language of Kvens when they moved to Norway, because Saami and Swedish loan words can also be found in northern dialects of Finnish and in Meänkieli. Still, the contacts between Kven and Saami speakers were intensified in Norway. The vocabulary of modern life has for the most part been borrowed from Norwegian, cf. [8] for a discussion.

The Kvens have undergone an assimilation process to Norwegian language and culture from late 19th century to late 1940's. The use of the Kven language was forbidden in schools and government offices. After the Norwegianization process the Kven language communities have gradually undergone a language shift, and most of the traditional areas now are monolingual Norwegian. The estimates of the number of speakers of Kven language vary from 2,000 to 8,000, depending on the criteria and methods used.

For political and historical reasons, the Kven language received the status of a minority language in 2005 within the framework of the European Charter for Regional or Minority Languages. Kven was recognized as a language, and not only as a dialect of Finnish. The national minority languages in Norway are protected by ECRML, which opens for protection on two levels and Kven language has been granted the lowest protection level, level II. The lowest level of protection obliges Norway to recognize the minority languages as an expression of cultural wealth, to promote and to protect them, to obtain forms and means for teaching and studies of minority languages, and to promote research of minority languages. Despite of these actions the language is still critically endangered.

The government's current heritage language policy is aimed at strengthening the Kven language in society. These actions include establishing the basic linguistic infrastructure for the language with the descriptive grammar, written standard and dictionaries. The work has been managed mainly by the Kven Institute, the national institution for the Kven language in Norway since 2007. Although the financial resources have been limited, the grammar of the Kven language was published in 2015.

3 Modeling phonology or morphophonology

3.1 The analyser

The Kven grammatical analyser is based on Eira Söderholm's descriptive grammar of Kven, *Kainun kielen grammatikki* [11], more specifically, the Porsanger variety of Kven (at least for the moment). The lexicon was originally taken from the dictionaries of Terje Aronsen [1] and Eira Söderholm [10], but it has later been completed by words taken partly from Kven informants and partly from corpus texts (`http://gtweb.uit.no/f_korp/`). An overview of the vocabulary is given in table 1.

Table 1: The vocabulary distribution across parts of speech

Nouns	Verbs	Adj	Closed	Names	Total
5,300	2,500	850	1,200	30,0000	≈ 40,000

The vocabulary is divided into 12 lexc files each consisting of all the lemmas, with stems and sublexica classification for each specific word type, as e.g. the entry for *amerikkalainen* 'American':

```
amerikkalainen:amerikkalai n_42 ;
```

The lexicon files contains 93 sublexica for categorizing the different stem types of the open parts of speech (34 for adjectives, 39 for nouns, and 23 for verbs). The parts of speech partly share the sublexica for representing derivational and inflectional suffixes, there are 210 such lexica.

In addition to the lexicon files there is a separate twolc file containing all the morphophonological changes possible within the stems (gemination, consonant gradation, and vowel shortening). This file includes the code for stem-final vowel or consonant changes, and for suffix changes like vowel harmony. The code compromises of 62 rules, with 128 context definitions for triggering.

The tagset is deliberately kept within mainstream Uralic descriptive linguistics, which means that it quite close to the bulk of the *Giellatekno* analysers. It deviates to a certain extent from the Omorfi analyser for Finnish, which is closer to the newer *ISO suomen kielioppi* (Finnish has e.g. `+InfA` and `+InfMa` where Kven has `+Inf` and `+Inf3`), but overall, the tagsets may be converted to each other.

3.2 Consonant gradation and vowel harmony

In the Finnic languages, consonant gradation (= cg) is seen as a process concerning
the plosives *k, p, t* The most concise presentation of the Finnish system to date is
. [5]). The same view has been held on other Finnic languages. A notable exception
has been Söderholm´s standard grammar of Kven. Here consonant gradation (*graadi-
vaihettelu,* op. cit. p.64ff) covers all the consonants *d, h, j, k, l, m, n, p, r, s, t* and *v.*
[11]. Söderholm unifies consonant gradation and what in Finnish dialectology has
been known as gemination, and thus gets a much broader gradation pattern, for more
consonants, more triggering contexts , and even an additional grade (e.g. *kk:k:j* for
lukkeet : lukenu : lujen 'to read, (has) read, I read´) for alternations that in Finnish
dialectology has been seen as gradation (*k : j*) and gemination (*k : kk*). The stem
for *lukkeet* in the system is thus *luke.* Söderholm knowingly treats gemination and
consonant gradation as the same, while we don't. These two processes have different
contexts and different realizations making it only logical from a technical point of
view to keep them separated.

Gradation is confined to *p, t, k,* whereas all consonants participate in gemination.
The process itself is simpler for gemination (a short consonant gets lengthened) than
for consonant gradation (which includes both quantitative and qualitative patterns).
Historically, consonant gradation was originally a phonological process: Long unvoiced geminates were shortened and short unvoiced ones were voiced in front of
closed syllables, *puku : puvun* 'coat'. This does not hold as a generalization in the
contemporary language, and consonant gradation is thus in transducers for Finnic
and Saami languages encoded as triggered by a special symbol ^WG inserted in the
lexc continuation lexicon rather than by referring to the closed syllable, like here for
$k : v$ (the left and right vowel contexts are specific in order not to overlap with the
$k : j$ and $k : 0$ gradation contexts. Also an example how inclusion is easier than
exclusion in twolc rules, as later mentioned in more details.)

```
"Gradation k:v"
k:v <=> [Vow - i] _ [o|ö|u|y] (:i) ^WG:0 ;

!! Test for this example:
!!€ puku^WG>n
!!€ puvu0>n
```

As a contrast, consider vowel harmony, which is treated as a phonological process. Consider the slightly simplified rule "Back harmony" below, where NonFront
is defined as any segment not in the set e i y ä ö ü æ ø, and BackVowel is defined as
a member of a o u å.

```
"Back harmony"
 Vx:Vy <=> BackVowel: NonFront:*  _ ;
         where Vx in ( %^A %^O %^U )
               Vy in (  a   o   u )
         matched ;
```

3.3   Gemination as insertion of consonant

As seen in the previous section, we treat consonant gradation morphologically (weak
grade is triggered by an explicit symbol ^WG rather than by a phonological context),
but vowel harmony we treat phonologically. When it comes to consonant gemination,
we are facing the same choice.

In Kven, a short consonant following a short stressed vowel becomes lengthened
when followed by a long vowel, like the nominative : partitive pair *sana* : *sannaa*
'word'. The lexc representation of the partitive form is sana>^V (i.e. the stem *sana*,
a suffix boundary and the partitive suffix ^V, or vowel copy. We have chosen to treat
this as a phonological process. The consonant gemination is thus treated in twolc as
a rule that doubles a given consonant in the context defined by the rule. For example
as follows:

```
"Consonant gemination for a"
0:Cx <=> Cx _ :a %>  :a ;
where Cx in  {đ h j k l m n p r s t v} ;
```

An alternative treatment would have been to avoid consonant insertion, by operating with a gemination place-holder in the stem instead, and by operating with a
trigger instead of relying upon the second syllable long vowel acting as a trigger. In
the alternative rule below, a dummy ^RC (root consonant) is changed to a copy of the
preceding consonant whenever followed by a lengthening trigger ^CNSLEN.

```
"Consonant gemination for a (alternative approach)"
%^RC:Cx <=> Cx _ ... %^CNSLEN: ;
```

In the lexicon file, this alternative approach would have been implemented as
follows: The gemination place-holder would have been added to all stems containing
a single root consonant, and all suffixes introducing a long second syllable would have
been enriched with the trigger symbol as well:

```
LEXICON Nouns
sana:san^RCa n_21 ;
```

```
...
LEXICON n_21
+Par:^CNSLEN%>^V K ; !  %^V = vowel copy
```

Our approach gives a more readable lexicon (the stem being *sana* rather than
san^RCa, at the expense of running the risk of introducing gemination in contexts
where it should not have been.

One might argue that using explicit triggers from lexc to twolc make the rules
easier to define (as the triggers are unique) and more easily maintainable than "implicit
triggers" that try to work with the letter itself.

3.4 Testing

We built a YAML test suite of hand-made conjugation paradigms for 54 nouns, 17
adjectives, 39 verbs and 2 pronouns, totaling 112 words. They where chosen so that
we at least had one representative for each of groupings of words in the reference
grammar [11]. These paradigms amount to 8,064 analysis and generation tests.

Since twolc rules are "global" in the sense that they actualize any time circumstances of the given context are fulfilled there is naturally a risk of false positives,
where there are other unforeseen circumstances that also match the rules' contexts
and the rule actualizes even though it shouldn't. Another challenge is when rules
have contexts that don't seem to overlap, until a word form comes up that fits into
both. There is a trade-off between having redundant, but clear and explicit lexc code
(increased amount of sublexica); and short and concise twolc where the complexity
is in narrowing down the contexts for the rules to only actualize in the instances you
want.

Creating a rule that matches a certain context is much simpler than making sure
there are no other conceivable contexts that also trigger the same rule. In other words,
including the context you want is easy, excluding the rest is difficult.

3.5 Practical applications

The analyser is already in use in several related projects. It has been used in the creation of a morphologically enhanced e-dictionary (`http://sanat.oahpa.no/fkv/`
`nob/`) and especially it's "point and click" functionality for translating words on any
website (see [3] for a presentation of the Kven dictionary, and [4] for a presentation of the dictionary platform), a Kven speller that may be downloaded for use in
LibreOffice or MS Word, and the publicly available e-learning tools Oahpa (`http:`
`//oahpa.no/kveeni`).

4 Evaluation

In the evaluation section, we look at lexical coverage, and discuss problems with text coverage for Kven. We then look at the grammatical coverage, i.e. to what extent it is able to analyze and generate the word forms of a representative set of Kven inflectional paradigms.

4.1 Evaluating text analysis

Kven is an *Ausbau* language, which means that from a former stage where Kven was not distinguishable from other Northern Finnish dialects, both Kven and Finnish have developed in different directions. Contemporary Kven writers are influenced by Finnish, and the Kven written norm that forms the foundation of the present analyser has a weak written tradition.

In order to evaluate the analyser, we tested it against the full Kven corpus[2], and against two subparts of it, one strictly adhering to the norm, and one consisting of texts taken from the Kven newspaper *Ruijan Kaiku*. For each of the 3 text collections, we give the coverage of the analyser, and for the words not recognized by the analyser, we indicate how large a part of these missing words are recognized by a Finnish analyser.[3]

Table 2: Coverage on different parts of the available corpus

Text type	Words	Coverage	Finnish OOV
Corpus adhering to norm	56,116	88.4 %	37.5 %
Contemporary news text	4,212	79.3 %	44.0 %
The full Kven corpus	260,375	84.9 %	40.1 %

The lowest coverage we get from the news material, the Kven periodical *Ruijan Kaiku*. Several of the words missing in the analyser are neologisms taken from the news domain, such as *minoritetti* 'minority', *standaarttii* 'standard', *elästytethään* 'revitalizes', while the dictionaries upon which the analyser was built have to a larger degree been geared towards the traditional language, as this is what most of the corpus has included. The newspaper was written in Finnish several years before starting

---

[2]The corpus is available at `http://gtlab.uit.no/f_korp/`

[3]The analysers are the ones found at http://victorio.uit.no/langtech/trunk/langs, the svn version used is r143378.

to write in Kven, and it is thus also no surprise that it has the highest percentage of Finnish among the words not known to the Kven analyser.

The coverage for the corpus adhering to norm is better, but still below 90 %. The reason for this is twofold. First, the text in question is a grammar ([11]), and as such it contains both scientific terminology, neologisms, affixes and dialect forms outside the standard. Second, the analyser still represents work in progress, and parts of both the morphophonology (especially the interplay between gemination and stem vowel changes linked to the $-i-$ suffix) and derivation are still not accounted for.

The non-recognized part of the corpus was also tested against a Norwegian analyser. We do not include any numbers for this, since the data was contaminated by conversion errors and citation loans, but the share of unassimilated Norwegian loans in the Kven text itself was small.

4.2   Evaluating grammatical paradigms

In order to test the morphological performance of the analyzer, we used the 8,064 word forms with their accompanying grammatical analyses, as described in section 3.4 above. The analyzer was tested both against analyzing and generating the set of word forms, and it returned 7,962 passes, or a correct percentage of 98.7 %.

Looking at the grammatical classification of Kven words found in the standard reference grammar [11], there are more tests than there are paradigm types in the grammar. In these tests, having at least one test set per LEXICON makes sense in the software engineering and unit test type of way, and having more than one examples makes it linguistically interesting. Therefore some classes are more heavily represented, the most obvious example of this over-representations are the continuation lexicon n_21 for which we have 7 yaml files, n_21ie for which we have 3, and n_31si for which we have 5. All these belong to the same class (nominal stem class 2.1 in the grammar), and (not coincidentally) these are some of the sublexica with the most amounts of words to them.

This over-representation should not have a significant impact on this tests performance, since the 3 lexemes with the most errors have 7 errors out of 159 inflectional forms, 6 out of 160 and 5 out of 159 errors. This implies that the errors are spread out evenly across the paradigms, so even if assuming the duplicated test (multiple tests for one class) where testing those we do better, the skew would be minor.

An example of a test suite is shown below.

```
[ 1/25][PASS] paivukko+N+Sg+Nom => paivukko
[ 2/25][PASS] paivukko+N+Sg+Gen => paivukon
...
```

```
[23/25][PASS] paivukko+N+Pl+All => paivukoile
[24/25][FAIL] paivukko+N+Pl+Ess => Missing results: paivukoina
[24/25][FAIL] paivukko+N+Pl+Ess => Unexpected results: paivukkoina
[25/25][FAIL] paivukko+N+Pl+Com => Missing results: paivukoine
[25/25][FAIL] paivukko+N+Pl+Com => Unexpected results: paivukkoine
-------------------------------------------------------------------

[ 1/25][PASS] paivukko => paivukko+N+Sg+Nom
[ 2/25][PASS] paivukon => paivukko+N+Sg+Gen
...
[23/25][PASS] paivukoile => paivukko+N+Pl+All
[24/25][FAIL] paivukoina => Missing results: paivukko+N+Pl+Ess
[25/25][FAIL] paivukoine => Missing results: paivukko+N+Pl+Com

Total passes: 46, Total fails: 4, Total: 50
```

5 Conclusion

In this article, we have presented an analyser for Kven. Although still containing flaws in both morphophonology, morphology and the lexicon, the analyser has a coverage of close to 90 % on normative Kven text, and has proved to be good enough to provide value when put to use in practical applications.

Linguistically, the stem list is kept maximally simple. This has made it easier for people without technical familiarity of the project to improve the lemma list. Consonant gradation is marked with a trigger in the morphology. The complicated system of root syllable consonant gemination is treated as a phonological process, so that a copy of the preceding consonant is inserted whenever the following vowel is long.

Kven as a standardised language is just in the making, with very few users adhering to the explicit written standard, a standard which is still not finalized. As a result of this, few text corpora may be seen as representing the norm, and language technology tools must be buildt with explicit normative statements, rather than upon analysing texts. A pleasant side effect of this it that the end result proves useful in a wide range of contexts.

With this set of architectural choices the Kven analyser is somewhat different from FST analysers for other Finnic and Saami languages, thereby offering an alternative approach to handling complex morphological properties of this type.

Acknowledgements

Thanks to Pirjo Paavalniemi for participating in initial work on the analyser, to Sjur Moshagen for building the infrastructure, to Lene Antonsen for comments to the twolc rules, and Hilde Skanke for providing a home for the project at Kainun Institutti. And last, but not least, we wanto to Eira Söderholm for writing a grammar we can build upon and for being available to discuss tricky nuances with the analysis.

References

[1] Terje Aronsen. *Kvensk-norsk-kvensk elektronisk ordbok.* Universitetet i Tromsø, 2010.

[2] Kenneth R. Beesley and Lauri Karttunen. *Finite State Morphology.* Studies in Computational Linguistics. CSLI Publications, Stanford, California, 2003.

[3] Mervi Haavisto, Kaisa Maliniemi, Leena Niiranen, Pirjo Paavalniemi, Tove Reibo, and Trond Trosterud. Kvensk ordbok på nett - hvem har nytte av den? *Skrifter / Nordisk forening for leksikografi,* 13:176–192, 2014.

[4] Ryan Johnson, Lene Antonsen, and Trond Trosterud. Using finite state transducers for making efficient reading comprehension dictionaries. In NEALT Proceedings Series, editor, *Proceedings of the 19th Nordic Conference of Computational Linguistics,* volume 16, pages 59–71, 2013.

[5] Fred Karlsson. *Suomen kielen äänne- ja muotorakenne.* WSOY, Juva, 1983.

[6] Kimmo Koskenniemi. *Two-level Morphology: A General Computational Model for Word-form Production and Generation,* volume 11 of *Yleisen kieliteteen laitos.* Helsingin yliopisto, Helsinki, 1983.

[7] Anna-Riitta Lindgren. *Miten muodot muuttuvat. Ruijan murteiden verbitaivutus Raisin, Pyssyjoen ja Annijoen kveeniyhteisössä.* Universitetet i Tromsø, Tromsø, 1993.

[8] Anna-Riitta Lindgren and Leena Niiranen. *The Morphological Integration of Scandinavian and Saami Verbal Borrowings in Kven and Their Impact on Contact-induced Language Change.* SKS, 2016.

[9] Sjur Moshagen, Jack Rueter, Tommi Pirinen, Trond Trosterud, and Francis M. Tyers. Open-source infrastructures for collaborative work on under-resourced

languages. In *Collaboration and Computing for Under-Resourced Languages in the Linked Open Data Era*, LREC, pages 71–77, Collaboration and Computing for Under-Resourced Languages in the Linked Open Data Era.

[10] Eira Söderholm. *Kainun sana- ja sanahaamulista Aikamatkaa varten*. Kvenfolket, http://kvenfolket.origo.no/-/page/show/2937_kvenskordliste, 2009.

[11] Eira Söderholm. *Kainun kielen grammatikki*, volume 1408 of *Suomalaisen kirjallisuuden seuran toimituksia*. SKS, Helsinki, 2014.

Author Index